Reuben Hatch

Bible Servitude Reexamined

Reuben Hatch

Bible Servitude Reexamined

ISBN/EAN: 9783744712576

Printed in Europe, USA, Canada, Australia, Japan

Cover: Foto ©Thomas Meinert / pixelio.de

More available books at **www.hansebooks.com**

BIBLE SERVITUDE RE-EXAMINED;

WITH

SPECIAL REFERENCE TO PRO-SLAVERY INTERPRETATIONS

AND

INFIDEL OBJECTIONS.

BY

REV. REUBEN HATCH, A.M.

"THY LAW IS THE TRUTH."—PSALMS.

CINCINNATI:
APPLEGATE & CO., PUBLISHERS,
No. 43 MAIN STREET.
1862.

CONTENTS.

CHAPTER I.

PAGE

ONE GREAT MISSION OF OUR AGE AND NATION............................   7

CHAPTER II.

THE GREAT MISTAKE... 10

CHAPTER III.

A PRIORI ARGUMENT.. 15

    SEC. 1.—Three Great Bible Facts... 15
    SEC. 2.—Chattel Slavery and the Law of Natural Right............. 16
    SEC. 3.—Chattel Slavery and the Great Law of Love................. 19
    SEC. 4.—Chattel Slavery makes the Bible Contradict Itself........ 23

CHAPTER IV.

DIRECT TESTIMONY OF THE BIBLE CONCERNING CHATTEL SLAVERY. 27

CHAPTER V.

BIBLE HISTORY AND TEACHING CONCERNING COMMON, OR NON-
    CHATTEL SERVITUDE.. 30

CHAPTER VI.

GENERAL VIEW OF PATRIARCHAL SERVITUDE........................... 32

    Stand-point 33
    Elements of the Patriarchal Household................................... 37

(iii)

CHAPTER VII.

PAGE

SPECIAL FACTS AND CONSIDERATIONS CONFIRMATORY OF THE FORE-
GOING CONCLUSION, THAT CHATTEL SLAVERY HAD NO PLACE IN
THE PATRIARCHAL HOUSEHOLDS.. 43

CHAPTER VIII.

PARTICULAR EXAMINATION OF VARIOUS PASSAGES OF SCRIPTURE
WHICH REFER TO PATRIARCHAL SERVITUDE........................... 58

SEC. 1.—Noah's Curse............... 58
SEC. 2.—Hagar... 65
SEC. 3.—Gen. xvii: 12, 27.. 72
SEC. 4.—Joseph... 76

CHAPTER IX.

A WONDERFUL AND SUBLIME PROPHECY................................... 88

CHAPTER X.

ANCIENT DARKNESS AND MODERN LIGHT—MODERN DARKNESS AND
ANCIENT LIGHT... 95

CHAPTER XI.

CONDITION OF THE JEWS IN EGYPT.. 96

CHAPTER XII.

THE MOSAIC CODE—Introduction... 100

CHAPTER XIII.

PARTICULAR EXAMINATION OF VARIOUS PASSAGES IN THE MOSAIC
CODE WHICH REFER TO SERVITUDE.. 102

SEC. 1.—Circumstances in which the Mosaic Code was given..... 102
SEC. 2.—Institution of the Passover.—Ex. xii: 43–47............. 104
SEC. 3.—Hebrew Servants.—Ex. xxi: 2–6............................ 107
SEC. 4.—Special case of Contract for Service and Anticipated
Marriage.—Ex. xxi: 7–11................................... 117
SEC. 5.—Sundry Regulations in regard to Servants.—Ex. xxi:
20, 21; xxi: 32; xxii: 3....................................... 127

CHAPTER XIV.

PAGE

FOREIGN SERVANTS—Analysis of Lev. xxv and xxvi.............. 134

CHAPTER XV.

THE JEWISH FAMILY THE TRUE MODEL.......................... 157

CHAPTER XVI.

NEW TESTAMENT TEACHING CONCERNING SERVITUDE................. 159

The Writers of the New Testament Jews—Hebrew and not Greek Writers—True Method of Understanding any Language—New Testament Usage Main Guide in Interpreting New Testament Language—Mistake of Conybeare and Howson—Classic Meaning of δοῦλος—New Testament Usage of δοῦλος—Inferences and Remarks.................. 159

CHAPTER XVII.

EXPOSITION OF PASSAGES IN THE NEW TESTAMENT WHICH SPEAK OF THE DUTIES OF MASTERS.................................... 176

Eph. vi: 9; Col. iv: 1.................................... 176

CHAPTER XVIII.

OF THE DUTIES OF SERVANTS................................ 184

SEC. 1.—Exposition of 1 Cor. vii: 20-24................... 184
SEC. 2.—Exposition of Eph. vi: 5-8....................... 192
SEC. 3.—Exposition of Col. iii: 22-25; iv: 1............. 198

CHAPTER XIX.

EXPOSITION OF 1 TIM. VI: 1, 2; AND TITUS, II: 9, 10......... 201

CHAPTER XX.

INFERENCES AND REMARKS SUGGESTED BY FOREGOING EXPOSITIONS. 206

CHAPTER XXI.

EXPOSITION OF 1 PETER, II: 18............................. 211

CONTENTS.

CHAPTER XXII.

PAGE

RECAPITULATION AND CONCLUSIONS.. 215

CHAPTER XXIII.

SPECIAL CHAPTER ON THE TWO RELATIONS (1) OF SERVANT AND
MASTER, AND (2) OF SLAVE AND OWNER................................... 223

CHAPTER XXIV.

REASON WHY SO FEW DIRECTIONS GIVEN TO MASTERS AND SERV-
ANTS—ON WHAT GROUND THESE DIRECTIONS ARE GOOD FOR
SLAVES AND SLAVEHOLDERS—SLAVEHOLDERS AND THE PRIMITIVE
CHURCHES.. 230

CHAPTER XXV.

SLAVERY AS A "SYSTEM," OR "INSTITUTION"........................... 236

CHAPTER XXVI.

ORIGIN OF SLAVERY.. 239

CHAPTER XXVII.

ONESIMUS.. 249

CHAPTER XXVIII.

BRIEF EXAMINATION OF SOME ANTI-SLAVERY VIEWS................. 261

SEC. 1.—Unhappy Translation of some Portions of the Bible
which relate to Servitude.. 261
SEC. 2.—The Bible Argument of Dr. Hopkins: Its Strength: Its
Weakness: Its Inconsistency................................. 263

CHAPTER XXIX.

BRIEF CRITICISMS UPON SOME OTHER ANTI-SLAVERY VIEWS......... 275

BIBLE SERVITUDE RE-EXAMINED.

CHAPTER I.

ONE GREAT MISSION OF OUR AGE AND NATION.

As the battle of the Lord Almighty in the contest between truth and error, right and wrong, goes on in the world, different ages and nations will occupy different portions of the field. Some of the ages, and some of the nations, will be thrown upon a mission of experiment and adventure: others will be convulsed with revolutions, bringing destruction to old systems of belief and practice: others, still, will be inspired to the work of repairing the old wastes, organizing, reconstructing, building up. It belongs especially to some of the ages to break up, and put to decay, that which has grown old, done its work, ripened off, and, in its own nature, is ready to vanish away. It is the special mission of some of the ages to discover, to shape, to lay foundations, and to build thereon that which can never be moved. There are ages of revolution, darkness, confusion, and chaos: and there are ages of quiet advancement in knowledge, science, and art, and in all ethical and spiritual

(7)

renovation and culture. Each has its place, its connections, its own work to do. They all help in carrying the world forward to a glorious millennium of truth and righteousness.

The whole mission of this wonderful present age can hardly be fully comprehended and stated by the living actors in it. Like all periods in the world's history, it is, undoubtedly, only partly known to itself.

If we do not mistake, it is a part of the mission of the present age *to settle the question of human liberty.* The providence of God has brought this question upon this age as a living question on both continents. It can not be suppressed: an irresistible providence is in it. The great God of the nations is putting the question, and opening humanity's great throbbing heart to entertain it, and act upon it. Thrones, principalities, and powers, Christian or heathen, royal or democratic, are utterly powerless to table it. Its discussion may darken the sun, and turn the moon into blood; it may shake the stars from their places in the heavens, as the figs are shaken from the fig-tree by untimely winds; nevertheless, it must go on, though in the midst of blood, and fire, and vapor of smoke. This is one of the great battles of this our age. It is already begun. The Armageddon of this battle is, and is to be, the American continent. Here slavery has reached its most terrible development: here it has established its stoutest throne: and here is to be the heart and heat of the contest.

The great Malakoff of slavery, deemed by its advocates absolutely impregnable, *is a pro-slavery interpretation of God's Bible*. To this it has retreated, and now bids defiance to all opposition. By this it has debauched the conscience of the world. By the help of this it has grown insolent and fierce, and now, at last, unblushingly seeks to degrade the laboring classes of all hues to the miserable condition of chattel slaves, *by divine authority*. It makes this demand by natural right, by Bible right, by all right. Further than this, indeed, it can not go: further than this it has no interest to go. But it means to hold all its ground *by divine authority*. Formerly, it condescended to bring meat-offerings to conscience and the Bible: now, at last, it has opened upon the human conscience the batteries of a pro-slavery interpretation of the Bible, and impudently demands a full surrender.

This brings the question of the Bible and slavery into the field: What are the relations of the Bible to slavery, and what are its teachings concerning it? If we are not mistaken, this is one of the important questions for this age to settle. This question has already been opened. It has been discussed: sometimes with a strange misapprehension of the facts, and with a logic stranger still; and sometimes with a powerful array of undeniable facts, and a strong logic. Manifest progress has been made. Many minds, however, still labor with this subject; and many totally mistake the tenor of Bible teaching concerning it. Commentators and Bible expounders have made grievous mistakes in interpreting the sacred oracles touching this subject.

We propose, in the following chapters, to make an humble, though earnest effort, to unfold the true relations and teachings of the Bible, both in regard to *free servitude* and *chattel slavery*. It is of the utmost importance, at the present time, that the American people should have clear and correct views on this whole subject, that they should be familiar with it, that individual conscience should be enlightened according to truth, and individual practice right. We humbly bespeak for these discussions a careful and candid perusal.

CHAPTER II.

THE GREAT MISTAKE.

ONE of the most unfortunate and grievous mistakes of modern literature is the pro-slavery interpretation which has been given to the Holy Bible. This mistake has been imposed especially upon the Patriarchal history, the Mosaic code, and those portions of the New Testament which give directions to servants and masters. The mistake in this interpretation has been in confounding the *free* or *non-chattel servitude* so frequently alluded to in the Sacred Scriptures, with *chattel slavery*, and in mistaking the former for the latter.

This mistake has been wide-spread. It runs through our Lexicons, Commentaries, Expositors, Histories, Law Books, School Books, Newspapers, Lectures, and Sermons. It is a base habit of modern literature to confound chattel slavery with Bible-approved servitude. It is not to our present purpose to inquire for the reasons of this. The fact can not be disputed.

. Now, we think it can be proved and shown, beyond all dispute or question, that the only servitude approvingly alluded to in any part of the Old or New Testament, was a *free* or *non-chattel servitude*, and, in no instance, *chattel slavery*. These are two very distinct and different things. It introduces endless mistakes, contradictions, and errors, to confound them in interpreting the Sacred Scriptures. To avoid this confusion in the present discussion, let us define and separate a little, in order that we may know whereof we are speaking.

Let it be carefully noted, in the first place, that *freedom* and *slavery* are not correlative terms. *Freedom* and *restraint* are correlatives. There may be a large measure of restraint without the least approach to slavery, and there may be a large measure of freedom along with slavery. In all civilized society there must be more or less restraint upon all the members thereof. But this is not slavery. In all human society, there must, of necessity, be more or less of servitude, and that more or less restricted. Parents must serve their children, and children their parents; teachers must serve their pupils, and pupils obey their teachers; ministers are bound to serve their people, and grateful people have the privilege of "ministering" to those by whom they are ministered unto, "in word and doctrine;" and all men are bound "by love" "to serve one another."

Let it be distinctly observed, also, that the word *slavery* has come to have a definite and very uniform meaning. Usage is much in advance of most of the dictionaries in its verdict as to the signification of this word. The word slavery, now describes the condition of human beings held or regarded as property. This is what slavery is in this country: this is the identical thing which constitutes the bone of contention and controversy between pro-slavery and anti-slavery men, and this is the sense in which the word is used with great uniformity, except in sophistical efforts of political demagogues and others to hide the true character of slavery. The slavery of this country is *chattel slavery*, and all the slavery there is in this country about which there is any controversy, is *chattel slavery*. Therefore, to avoid all ambiguity, we shall use the term *slavery*, and the compound term *chattel slavery*, in the sense indicated above.

We will endeavor to remember, then, what chattel slavery is, and what it is not.

1. It is not governmental oppression of free men. There may be, and often is, much of this, more or less unjust and wicked, without any approach to chattel slavery.

2. It is not individual oppression of servants, paid

or unpaid. This is everywhere common enough, and always has been, but does not constitute chattel slavery.

3. It is not social oppression of classes of people whose circumstances are providentially unfortunate, either through their own vices and follies, or tho misfortunes and misdeeds of their ancestors; or neither. Abundant examples of this, involving great wrong, are to be found in our large cities.

4. Nor again, is it the punishment of criminals for their crimes. This may involve close confinement and hard labor, for others without compensation, but does not constitute chattel slavery.

5. Nor yet is it restriction of rights and privileges on account of peculiar circumstances. Foreigners, under any government, may be circumscribed in their privileges very much, and yet by no means reduced to a state of chattel slavery.

6. The rendering of service without remuneration, which service is even rendered with great reluctance, is not, and does not constitute chattel slavery.

7. Unqualified subordination to unlimited authority, as in the case of sailors on board of ships, and as was the condition of children in relation to their fathers among the old Romans, does not make chattel slavery.

8. Filial subordination and subjection does not constitute chattel slavery.

9. Apprenticeship is not chattel slavery.

10. Moral and spiritual enslavement to appetite, lust, and passion, is not chattel slavery.

There may be great oppression and great wickedness connected with any or all of these things, and
others like them, yet in no such things as these is
chattel slavery to be found. The oppression in them
is the oppression of people unchattelized, and there
is neither slave nor slavery in them.

It will bear to be repeated: chattel slavery is the
chattelizing of human beings—*it is the regarding,
treating, and holding of human beings as property.*
The oppressing of free people, whether they be servants, masters, or kings, however wicked and wrong
it may be, is not chattel slavery. The restricting
of the privileges of people, for adequate reasons in
the circumstances, is not chattel slavery. Chattel
slavery is the propertyizing of human beings. This
is its prime, essential element. This is what constitutes the burden, the entity of the thing. It is
the same when imposed upon a king, as when imposed upon a servant: it is the same when imposed
upon a black man as when imposed upon a white man.
As a practical fact, it stands alone in the world: in
all our investigations and reasonings concerning it,
let us keep it isolated and separated from every thing
else. Especially let us endeavor to keep it distinct
from *free* or *non-chattel servitude.* This latter servitude, more or less restricted, the Bible recognizes,
provides for and makes laws for; the other, chattel
slavery, it knows nothing of except to condemn and
prohibit it. Free or non-chattel servitude, more or
less restricted, is a benevolent necessity of human
society; chattel slavery, wherever it prevails, is its

direst curse. The former the Bible recognizes and sanctions; the latter it condemns and prohibits. This, a careful examination of Patriarchal history, the Mosaic code, and those portions of the New Testament which give instructions to servants and masters, will, we think, abundantly show.

CHAPTER III.

A PRIORI ARGUMENT.

SECTION 1.—*Three Great Bible Facts.*

IN opening the Bible, as God's book, three great facts stand revealed before us.

1. As God's book, the Bible is, and must be, consistent with itself. All its particular precepts and injunctions must be in perfect harmony with its fundamental principles: and all these must be in harmony with one another.

2. All the teachings of the Bible must agree with the great law of love: since, on the authority of the great Teacher himself, this law lies at the foundation of all that the Bible contains. There is, and can be, nothing in the Bible, which God has sanctioned, inconsistent with this law.

3. As God's book, the Bible must be consistent with the law of natural right.

Indeed, the law of natural right is nothing else

than the great law of love, as announced in the Sacred Scriptures.

No man in his senses can deny any of these statements. If the Bible is God's book, it must be consistent with itself: it must be consistent with the great law of love : it must be consistent with natural right. Any interpretation which makes the Bible contradict itself, any interpretation which makes its teachings inconsistent with the great law of love, any interpretation which brings it into conflict with the law of natural right, must be false.

Thus far, all is clear, on the supposition that the Bible is God's book. If, then, chattel slavery, or any thing else, makes the Bible contradict itself, the Bible does not, and can not, sanction it, or that thing : if chattel slavery, or any thing else, makes the Bible violate the law of love, which is professedly its own fundamental principle, the Bible does not, and can not, sanction it, or that thing : if chattel slavery, or any thing else, brings the Bible into conflict with the law of natural right, the Bible does not, and can not, sanction it, or that thing.

These conclusions are inevitable.

SEC. 2.—*Chattel Slavery and the Law of Natural Right.*

Let us, then, in the first place, confront chattel slavery, face to face with the law of natural right. Chattel slavery, mark, is the chattelizing of human beings. The property-element is that which distinctively characterizes and constitutes it. As a matter of fact, this element lies at the foundation of all slave-holding enactments, of all fugitive slave laws, of all judicial decisions on the side of slavery, and of all pro-slavery reasonings relating thereto.

And to call chattel slavery a mere paternal guardianship, or to give it any other smooth and innocent name, is the most paltry and shallow quibbling to which partisan sycophancy or cotton divinity ever descended. Chattel slavery is the reducing of human beings to the category of property. Now, this is nothing else and nothing less than direct and gross trespass upon inalienable, personal, natural rights.

It is a somewhat which no human being ever has, or ever can have, the least right to do to his fellow. I have not, and by no possibility can I ever have, the least imaginable right to hold or treat my neighbor as property: and he has not, and never can have, any right to regard, or hold, or treat me as property. No combination of men, no extent of governmental authority has any such right. The right can not exist any more than the right to regard, hold, or treat human beings as brutes can exist. There is no power in heaven, earth, or hell, so great as to possess the right to regard, hold, and treat human beings, God-made above the brutes, and God-imaged, as brutes. No such right is either possible or allowable. To do so is direct personal wrong, *per se*, to those so held and regarded. Exactly in the same way, and for the same reason, the right to chattelize human beings never did, and never can, exist. It is direct trespass upon rights that inhere in universal human-

ity.   It is gross wrong, and can never be perpetrated without involving gross wrong.   It is always
sin *per se*, and no times, places, or circumstances can
make it any thing else.   It is always unlawful and
forbidden trespass upon that manhood which never
deserts a living, breathing child of Adam.

And this is *the verdict of universal conscience.*
There is not a living man on the face of the earth,
whose manhood has not been crushed out of him by
gross abuse, who would not instantly know and feel
himself greatly wronged, in the first attempt of his
fellow to treat him as property.   Every living conscience knows absolutely that this is trespass upon
God-given manhood, and palpable violation of the
great law of natural right.   There is not a slaveholder in all slaverydom that does not know this;
and whose moral sense, when the hellish screws of
this degradation should be wrenched down upon himself, would not be startled and offended, and cry out,
with unmistakable authority, *" Hands off !"*

So testifies universal humanity.   Indeed, there is
not a plainer violation of the great law of natural
right perpetrated under the light of the sun, nor in
the hidden darkness of midnight, than the chattelizing of human beings.   To chattelize the infant in
the cradle, is to violate its Adamic manhood: it is
trespass upon the sacred dignity of its living and
distinctive creatureship as coming from God Almighty's hand.   It can no more be done without
wrong, than you can regard your brother as a dumb
brute, or treat him maliciously and selfishly, without

wrong. To chattelize the full-grown man or woman, is direct trespass upon natural and inherent rights, and can never be perpetrated without sin, and that too, *sin per se*, even though done to the meanest wretch that ever lived, and in the deepest bosom of the lowest depths of the bottomless pit. It is pure sin always and everywhere, and neither man nor devil can make it any thing else, any more than the malicious and selfish treatment of God's rational creatures can be made any thing else than sin.

Therefore, by the surest sequence, since the Bible, as God's book, does not and can not sanction any thing that violates the law of natural right, and since, as we have seen, chattel slavery is palpable and gross trespass upon the law of natural right; the Bible does not, and can not, give it any countenance whatever.

SEC. 3.—*Chattel Slavery, and the Great Law of Love.*

The Bible, as God's indivisible revelation of truth to man, has its fundamental principle of law and doctrine. That principle is the law of love.

This is not only the great principle which underlies the whole Bible, and upon which all its teachings, from Genesis to Revelation, rest, but it is also the great fundamental principle of the entire moral government of God. The first and simplest expansion of this principle is that made by Jesus Christ: "Thou shalt love the Lord thy God with all thy heart;" and, "Thou shalt love thy neighbor as thyself." On this moral couplet "hang all the law and

the prophets;" and it may now be added, with perfect truthfulness, all the gospel too. This is the
divine announcement of the one great law of love:
love as a principle of action—love which is true benevolence—love which is good-will to being, unselfish, impartial, universal. This principle covers all
possible right, and, by implication, interdicts all possible wrong. With this principle the entire Bible
harmonizes, and never departs from it in any of its
laws, doctrines, instructions, or precepts. Every
word that proceedeth out of the mouth of the Lord,
on all moral questions and subjects, must be based
on this principle, and agree with it.

This principle, therefore, is always a safe guide in
the study and interpretation of the Bible, so far as
we are able to understand and apply it. Any interpretation of the Bible which can be fully and fairly
shown to be in conflict with this principle, must, of
necessity, be wrong. Any interpretation which ar-
rays God's teachings, arrangements, permissions, or
admissions, in regard to the social relations of Jews
or Gentiles, against this principle, must be erroneous.

Now this principle, be it remembered, recognizes
and protects all rights, and forbids all trespass upon
rights. It demands that every being shall be considered and treated benevolently, and all his rights
sacredly regarded. It protects all rights, and condemns all trespass upon rights. Hence it does and
forever must recognize and defend the individual
and personal manhood of every child of Adam. It
allows no trespass upon that manhood or any of its

rights. For example, it does not, and it can not, allow that rational creatures, made in the divine image, should be regarded and treated as brutes. It does not allow this from fellow creature; it does not allow it from angel; it does not allow it from God. Such treatment is both a lie and a direct trespass upon inherent, unalienated, and unalienable rights. Hence, by no possibility can the law of love ever allow any such thing. It must eternally condemn it.

Nor again, example second, does this law permit either God or man to treat the creature maliciously and selfishly. Neither devils in perdition, nor wicked criminals of earth, can be treated by any being, or combination of beings, maliciously and selfishly, without direct violation of the great law of love. All such treatment is sin *per se*, sin in itself, and nothing but sin. Criminals may be punished, but always for adequate reasons, and at the behests of the law of love. No being can be, or become, so guilty as to be beyond the circle of the great law of good-will. Even devils have a sacred creatureship, which ill-will can not invade without rebuke and condemnation from the great moral law of the universe. Then, surely, this must be true of angels and probationary men.

In like manner, example third, the chattelizing of human beings is, in itself, a direct violation of the great law of love. From the statements and explanations already made, this is perfectly manifest. Chattel slavery, as we have seen, is direct trespass upon inherent, unforfeited, and unforfeitable rights, and hence, since the law of love eternally forbids such trespass, it must be only and simply violation of that law.   Good-will to my neighbor never does, and never can, lead me to invade sacred and inalienable rights. If, by crime, he forfeits certain rights and privileges, neither by crime nor by any thing else can he forfeit his right to manhood.   This right is absolutely inalienable.   It lies wholly beyond the reach of forfeiture. No being in the universe can trench upon this right, without trampling under foot the Scripture law of love.   Chattel slavery lays hold of this right, and lays it in the dust; hence it tramples down the great law of love; and hence, again, it must be contrary to all Scripture, for all Scripture, both general and particular, agrees perfectly with this law.

This reasoning is so simple, so plain, so conclusive, so unanswerable, that more words need not be expended to make it plainer.   The Scripture law of love must forever interdict all chattelizing of human beings.   And, in spite of all learned logomachy to make something else appear, I verily believe the Christian, moral sense of the world does so decide. The best piety of the Christian world does not judge that the law of love sets men to chattelizing, enslaving, their fellow beings: that such nefarious invasion of unforfeited and inalienable rights is a beautiful, heavenly, and Christ-like exemplification and fruit of disinterested, unselfish, pure, and holy love!   It never has judged thus, and it never will, for the very good reason that such judgment is a lie.

SEC. 4.—*Chattel Slavery makes the Bible contradict itself.*

It follows inevitably, from the foregoing reasonings and conclusions, that the Bible can not give any sanction to chattel slavery without loading itself with endless contradictions. The following examples will sufficiently illustrate and confirm this remark:

1. The Bible, as all that read it well know, every-where condemns *all oppression* in the strongest language, and never spares its terrible threatenings of the most fearful judgments upon the oppressor. God's rebuke against oppression, in all forms, as gross sin and gross violation of the divine law, literally runs through the entire Bible. Moses wrote: "Thou shalt not defraud thy neighbor, neither rob him;"* "Thou shalt neither vex a stranger nor oppress him;"† "Ye shall not oppress one another;"‡ "Thou shalt love thy neighbor as thyself;"§ and much more of the same import. He frequently refers the Jews to their own experience under the hand of the oppressor in the land of Egypt, as teaching them to "know the heart of a stranger," as a strong motive to deter them from practicing oppression upon their fellow-beings, even though they were strangers and Gentiles. The command is most express, and oft repeated throughout the Pentateuch, to the Jews, that they should "do no unrighteousness" either to "neighbor" or "stranger."

Now, who does not know that there is no oppression

* Lev. xix: 13 † Ex. xxii: 21. ‡ Lev. xxv: 14, 17. § Lev. xix: 18.

done under the sun more unrighteous, *more oppres-sive*, more grievous to be borne, more unlawful and outrageous, than that which begins by trampling the very manhood of the rational creature in the dust, and continues only by a continuous perpetration of the same villainous trespass upon God-given rights? Who does not know that this is the highest kind of robbery? There is no other robbery that can be perpetrated upon a human being, that deprives him of so much that is good and valuable to him, as that involved in chattelizing him. It implies in it univer-sal trespass upon all rights. It is the perfection of oppression upon men, to reduce them to the condition of property, and use them as such. Everybody knows this. And the man that does not know this, or pre-tends that he does not, only needs to be put under this terrible millstone of wrong to bring him fully to his senses.

Therefore, if Moses has anywhere given any sanc-tion to chattel slavery, either among Jews or Gentiles, he has flatly contradicted himself. He has both for-bidden all oppression and sanctioned the most abom-inable and unlawful stamp of oppression that ever cursed the earth. This contradiction can be obviated only by denying that chattel slavery *is* oppression, which is a manifest falsehood, or by denying that Moses does sanction it, which latter assertion both is, and can be shown to be, the truth.

In like manner, the prophets, and the writers of the New Testament, abound in the strongest denun-ciations of oppression and the oppressor, the language of which is oftentimes most terrific. All along, either expressly or implicitly, God promises to "be a swift witness" "against those that oppress the hireling in his wages, the widow and the fatherless, and that turn aside the stranger from his right."* How complete the contradiction, if, through these writers, in the same breath, God has given warrant for that which is the climax of all oppressions! admitted and known to be such by the universal, moral sense of the race!

2. Again, multitudes of *particular precepts* utterly subvert chattel slavery, and make it impossible. Quotations under this head might be extended to fill a volume. Examples abound on almost every page of the Bible. Only one or two, however, can be given here. "Thou shalt love thy neighbor as thyself." No man can obey this command, in its true spirit, and make merchandise of his neighbor.

"Masters give unto your servants that which is just and equal." No master can do that, and, at the same time, regard, and treat, and hold his servants as property. No man can, for a moment, hold his servants as chattel slaves, without perpetrating the grossest injustice: no man can do it without subverting all righteous equality. By no possibility can any one hold any but free servants, in obedience to this precept.

In like manner, multitudes of other particular precepts of the Bible run directly under chattel slavery, subverting it utterly. Obedience to these

* Mal. iii : 5.

3

precepts is altogether incompatible with the chattelizing of our brother man.

3. The Bible *expressly forbids* chattel slavery, under
penalty of death, and so can nowhere give it sanction
without flatly contradicting its own positive injunctions.   "If a man be found stealing any of his brethren of the children of Israel, and maketh merchandise
of him, or selleth him; then that thief shall die;
and thou shalt put evil away from among you."—
Deut. xxiv: 7.   Beyond all contradiction, the thing
forbidden here is *chattel slavery:* it is treated as an
evil, (a moral evil,) to be put away: the man who
should be guilty of this evil is pronounced a "thief:"
the penalty for such theft is capital punishment,
showing that the crime is a capital one.

Now, if any one demurs from all this, by saying
that this law related only to the chattelizing of Jews,
he is respectfully but earnestly referred to the general
statute in Ex. xxi: 16, under which the specific enactment in Deuteronomy belongs.   "And he that
stealeth a man and selleth him, or if he be found in
his hand, he shall surely be put to death."   "A man"
—any man.   This is "the law," which Paul affirms
in 1 Tim. i: 10, was made for "men-stealers."   Here
then, we have, first in God's Bible, the universal
statute forbidding chattel slavery on pain of death:
and second, lest the Jews should overlook a command
so important, a specific statute guarding every Jew
in particular, as the general statute guarded every
man of the race, from this most ruinous and grievous
of all violations of the second table of the great law

of love.   In both cases alike, the crime is considered a capital offense, with capital punishment for its penalty.   Chattel slavery can begin, and can be perpetuated only by man-stealing, and making merchandise of those so stolen.   Man-stealing is in it, every moment of its existence.   If the Bible allows this, it allows that which is a manifest contradiction of its own express injunctions.

CHAPTER IV.

DIRECT TESTIMONY OF THE BIBLE CONCERNING CHATTEL SLAVERY.

PRECISELY in accordance with the foregoing statements, reasonings, and conclusions, is the direct and positive testimony of the Bible concerning chattel slavery.   With earnest and solemn emphasis, it catalogues it, as we have just seen, as a crime—and as a capital crime.   This testimony is brief, but unequivocal, decisive, and conclusive.   Great and gross crimes are frequently disposed of in God's Scripture in few words.   There are iniquities on this earth of which, the pen of inspiration declares, it is a shame even to speak.

This direct and express testimony of the Bible concerning chattel slavery is not to be found, however, in either Old or New Testament legislation concerning free or non-chattel servitude.   Entirely separate from this, it stands by itself alone.   It is testimony which fully grapples with the subject, and disposes of it at once.

Of chattel slavery, God said to the Jews, by the mouth of their great law-giver, Moses: "And he that stealeth a man, and selleth him, or if he be found in his hand, he shall surely be put to death." —Ex. xxi: 16.

But lest the Jews should overlook a command so important, this general statute is reiterated in a specific form, to guard every Jew in particular, as the general statute guarded every individual of the race, from this most ruinous and grievous of all violations of the second table of the great law of love. "If a man be found stealing any of his brethren of the children of Israel, and maketh merchandise of him, or selleth him; then that thief shall die; and thou shalt put evil away from among you."—Deut. xxiv: 7.

Comment upon these passages is hardly necessary. There is no mistaking the subject spoken of in these passages: there is no mistaking that which is said. They contain the sum and substance of Mosaic legislation on the subject of chattel slavery.

This legislation seems to have been anticipatory, and designed to meet individual cases of crime of this sort, that might possibly arise in the future history of the Jews. It contemplates no existing system of iniquity, inasmuch as no such system was in existence when these statutes were delivered. It is brief, positive, and final. Bible prophets, preachers, and historians recognize this as God's authoritative legislation on this subject.

This legislation is distinctly alluded to and indorsed by the great apostle and leading writer of the New Testament, in the following passage: "But we know that the law is good, if a man use it lawfully; knowing this, that the law is not made for a righteous man, but for the lawless and disobedient, for the ungodly and for sinners, for unholy and profane, for murderers of. fathers and murderers of mothers, for man-slayers, for whoremongers, for them that defile themselves with mankind, for men-stealers, for liars, for perjured persons, and if there be any other thing contrary to sound doctrine."—1 Tim. i: 8, 9, 10.

The "law" referred to in this passage is, unquestionably, the law of Moses. That particular portion of it which was "made" "for men-stealers" must be the identical statutes which we have quoted above. Hence, the apostle fully indorses the Mosaic law concerning chattel slavery. It is especially worthy of remark concerning this passage, that the word "*men-stealers*" means, etymologically, *men-sellers*, or properly, *enslavers*, showing that Paul distinctly recognized the stealing and selling as one and the same offense."*

We have, then, the direct, positive testimony of both Testaments concerning chattel slavery as great and gross crime, unequivocally and positively forbidden. The law of natural right, the great law of love, and the express, positive testimony of the Bible are perfectly agreed in their verdict concerning it.

* Pres. E. B. Fairfield.

CHAPTER V.

BIBLE HISTORY AND TEACHING CONCERNING COMMON OR NON-CHATTEL SERVITUDE.

THE foregoing statements, reasonings, and conclusions have never yet been met, face to face, and shown to be faulty or erroneous. They never can be. Nevertheless, the advocates of chattel slavery, and multitudes of others, imagine that, somehow, all this is set aside as containing some hidden fallacy, by the supposed fact that certain particular precepts and laws in the Bible do recognize and sanction the existence of chattel slavery; that they were designed by the Almighty to regulate it as an admissible and lawful institution; and that when, as a matter of fact, it is so regulated, it is, for the time being, at least, lawful and right, and receives the Divine approbation.

In this false notion lies the great mistake in interpreting the teachings of the Bible concerning chattel slavery. As already observed, this mistake consists in confounding chattel slavery with righteous, non-chattel servitude, and in interpreting the teachings of the Bible concerning the latter as if they related to the former. In this way these entire teachings have been wrested and abused to the service of chattel slavery: in this way God's freely-expressed sanction of common, or non-chattel servitude, has been stolen for the expressly prohibited iniquity of chattel slavery. In this way divine sanction for chattel slavery has been found in the righteous, non-chattel servitude of the Patriarchs, in the laws and regulations of the Mosaic code concerning common servitude, and in the teachings of the New Testament on the same subject. By this falsehood, as the cuckoo appropriates the nest of her neighbor in which to incubate and nestle her own young, chattel slavery has found a nesting place in God's Word. Nowhere else in the Divine Word is to be found a place even for the sole of its foot. It maintains its place here only by false interpretation, and by arraying one portion of the Bible against other portions.

This makes it necessary to examine the whole subject of common or non-chattel servitude, as that subject is alluded to and treated of in the Sacred Scriptures. We propose to prosecute this examination under the three following heads, in their order, namely, Patriarchal Servitude, Mosaic Servitude, and New Testament Servitude. In no one of these shall we find chattel slavery. The true title, therefore, of this examination is, " Bible History and Teaching concerning Common, or Non-chattel Servitude."

CHAPTER VI.

GENERAL VIEW OF PATRIARCHAL SERVITUDE.

In the history of the Patriarchs, as given by Moses, allusions to servitude frequently appear. This is as might have been expected: for, as already intimated, servitude, of necessity, belongs to all human society, and probably to all society of good and holy beings in heaven and everywhere else. Indeed, what is obedience to the great law of love, other than heartily willing, and sincerely doing, service for others? What an indefatigable servant to the universe which his benevolence has built, is the great Father of all! The Lord Jesus Christ, the great representative of the Father, came into this world "not to be minis- tered unto"—not to receive service—but "to minis- ter," to render service. And are not the angels "all ministering spirits" — serving messengers — "sent · forth" to do service "for them who shall be heirs of salvation?" In the church of Christ, too, the great law is, "by love serve one another."

Indeed, service-rendering is the noblest form of rational and moral activity. In the very constitution of human society there must be service, compensated or uncompensated, servitude in different forms. In the early history of the race, before the flood, and on after the flood in Patriarchal times, there was servi- tude, of course. Servitude, in some form, more or

:ess restricted, is to be looked for in all ages of the world, and in all places where human beings dwell. But this, by no means, implies the existence of chattel slavery. This is often assumed, but always without good reason. The having of servants is one thing; the chattelizing of servants, or of other people, is quite another thing.

The question, therefore, for us to keep in mind all along in this examination of Patriarchal servitude, is not whether servitude actually existed in the families of Abraham and the Patriarchs, for this is fully admitted; but whether the servitude which existed there was the servitude of *freemen*, or the servitude of *chattel slaves*. A true view of Patriarchal servitude will show that it must have been the former, and could not possibly have been the latter.

Stand-point.

In looking in upon the social relations, and in examining the condition of the different members of Patriarchal society, it is all-important to gain the right stand-point. If we assume, to start with, that Abraham, who lived nearly four thousand years ago, was located on some modern South Carolina negro plantation, and that the forms of language and expression in which his history is given were derived from the usages, feelings, and prejudices of modern pro-slavery society, we make a great mistake. This at once puts us into a false position in relation to Patriarchal servitude, and the view gained therefrom is false.

4

Abraham and the Patriarchs, it should be remembered, lived only a few generations after the flood. They lived in *simple, Patriarchal times*, when the earth was just beginning to be inhabited, when a nation consisted either of a mere family, with the father at the head, as ruler, or, at most, of a small tribe or clan, with the leading patriarch thereof at the head, as chief, or king. Of necessity, this must have been the state of things for several generations after the flood ; and for a long time after, there must have been a strong tendency to this Patriarchal form of government and of society. Now this was a state of society and a form of government somewhere between the simple, single family model and a kingdom. Kingdoms, in the enlarged modern sense, had not yet appeared. The Patriarch, or chief, was not a king after the fashion of modern kings, but was rather the ruling head of a *compound family*.

The first generation after the flood consisted of Japheth, Shem, and Ham, and their wives: three families. The second consisted of the children of these three great sires of the post-diluvian world, and a corresponding number of families. As succeeding generations followed, families were multiplied. In the tenth after the flood, Abraham lived. Now, it is very manifest, that in this early period of the settlement of the earth, in this Patriarchal age, people must have dwelt apart, as separate and independent families, or they must have associated themselves together, either in one single community, or in several smaller communities, according to relationships, tastes, or other circumstances. But it is very easy to see that human beings, in any age of the world, would not be very likely to dwell "alone," either as single individuals, or as isolated families. They would naturally seek association together. The power of the *social principle* alone, would be sufficient to draw them together, either in one general community, or into smaller compound households or tribal communities. So, too, from considerations of mutual convenience in getting a living, as herdsmen, hunters, and tillers of the ground, and for purposes of mutual defense against wild beasts, and against other clans, or individuals, would they be brought together in the same way. All the history that has come down to us of those early times confirms these statements.

It is further manifest, that leading minds would be very likely to establish households of their own, and gather about them other families and individuals of less mental and physical power, and so become heads, chiefs, or patriarchs of the tribes, or little kingdoms, thus constituted. Hence the multiplication of tribes and chiefs in Patriarchal times. And hence each compound, patriarchal household would be made up of the Patriarch's own family proper, and of other single families, and individuals, male or female, associated with him.

In all cases the Patriarch, or chief, was the acknowledged leader and ruler. In him, for the most part, was vested the supreme governmental authority, as law-giver, judge, and general. Of the whole com-

pound household he was principal master. All the
members thereof acknowledged his authority as head-
man, and held themselves ready to follow him, and
perform any service which he should require. He
was lord and master of the whole household, and
all its members accounted themselves his servants.
Nevertheless, this apparently absolute authority
would be strongly restrained and much controlled
by the Patriarch's own sense of justice, and by the
will and wishes of the members of his tribe. Of
course, before inferiority of races was either known or
possible in the world, such association of families and
individuals would be entirely voluntary, and on the
principle of fundamental equality. On the ground
of governmental necessity, the Patriarch was head-
man of the whole household, but head-man by the
free consent of the individual members thereof. In
the nature of the case, without such consent, he would
be utterly powerless. He was head-man over a community of freemen, and all his power lay in their
voluntary devotion to him and the household. It
would seem that chattel slavery, in such circumstances, would be an absolute impossibility. Says an
eminent Southern senator: "Slavery can not exist a
day or an hour, in any Territory or State, unless it
has affirmative laws sustaining and supporting it,
furnishing police regulations, and remedies," any
more "than a new-born infant could survive under
the heat of the sun, on a barren rock, without protection." Who can not see that such supports of
law and police force would be impossible in the little

independent Patriarchal tribes or households into which the race were gathered in the Patriarchal ages following the flood, including Abraham's day? It seems to us that the very constitution of society utterly forbade the existence of chattel slavery in those days. A *correct view* of Patriarchal society reveals the fact that chattel slavery was impossible, and that the servitude of those days was simply the servitude of honorable citizenship in the household.

Elements of the Patriarchal Household.

The manner in which the Patriarchal household was thus made up and enlarged, reveals very clearly the different elements, or sorts of persons, of which it was composed. It is manifest from Scripture, as well as from other ancient history, that it was regarded, in Patriarchal times, as a matter of great importance to enlarge and strengthen the household, or tribe, as much as possible. Indeed, in those days, when land and many other things which constitute modern property, were of little or no value, a man's possessions were estimated mostly by the extent of his household, and the number of his cattle and sheep. Hence it was always a favorite object with the Patriarch to gather about him a numerous household. A large citizenship was his pride and delight. This fact frequently crops out in Scripture and other ancient history.

The Patriarch could accomplish this in several ways: but always on the principle of freedom. In the circumstances of those early times, it would

plainly be impossible for him to make up and enlarge
his household on the basis of chattel slavery.   In the
nature of the case, his whole power lay in the voluntary devotion of the members of his household.   There
was no police force, military power, or governmental
authority whatever back of them, to which he could
appeal or resort for the enforcement of his commands.
Foreign aid, from beyond the circle of his own little
community, was entirely out of the question.   Voluntary loyalty to himself and the household was the sole
basis of all his power.   In such a state of things,
chattel slavery was manifestly impossible.   As things
actually were, in Patriarchal times, when the people
were few, and the materials for the formation of nations with the machinery of national governments
did not exist, when the earth all lay common and
open to every man, when inferiority of races and
most of the artificial distinctions of modern society
were unknown, and when all the people were much
on a level as to intellectual, moral, and social culture,
it would have been a simple impossibility for any
Patriarch or chief to make up a household, to enlarge
and strengthen it, or to keep it together on the basis
of chattel slavery.   Isolate Southern slave plantations, cut them off from all help of police force and
other governmental support from without, lay out
the whole country, teeming with game and vegetable
productions for the support of human life, common
and open to every man, abolish the idea of inferiority
of races, and introduce the equality of ancient Patriarchal days between slave and master, as to education,

moral development, social culture, general intelligence, and common habits, and chattel slavery could not exist a single day.

The construction and enlargement of the Patriarchal household, therefore, could have proceeded only on the basis of free, honorable, and voluntary citizenship. On this basis the embryo kingdom of the Patriarch might have been enlarged in several ways.

1. First, obviously, by natural increase: embracing his own children, grand-children, etc., and close kindred.

2. By mutual agreement: whereby several families became associated together, subject to one Patriarch or chief. It would always be an advantage, in many ways, for inferior families to join superior and stronger households.

3. The Patriarch might also build up and enlarge his household by a mutual contract or bargain for service and citizenship in the household, for a given sum of money paid by him. This bargain might be for a limited or an unlimited period of time. The Patriarch might thus "buy" citizens for his tribe or embryo kingdom for a term of years, for life, or forever. When the time was unlimited, the individuals thus engaged by Patriarchal purchase, would become united to the household as their nation and home, permanently: much as modern emigrants leave one nation and settle in another permanently for themselves and their children, except that in Patriarchal days the nation was only a large household.

4. Another source of enlargement would be from children born within the range of the general household. In this gathering together of families and individuals to make up the Patriarchal compound or tribal household, single families remained intact, and single family relations undisturbed. Nevertheless, these families, as parents and children, belonged to, and made part and parcel of, the tribe. Children born in any part of the tribe, just as in nations at the present day, belonged to the tribe, and added to its strength.

Patriarchal society, therefore, would contain in it the following fundamental elements:

1. Children proper, and near kindred.

2. Individuals and families associated by mutual negotiation.

3. Individuals and families bought with money.

4. Children born in any department of the general household.

Guests, strangers, and sojourners, and hired servants, being transient persons in relation to the household, are, of course, omitted in this enumeration of fundamental elements.

If, now, we turn to the history of the Hebrew Patriarchs, as given us in the Bible, we shall find, as a matter of fact, that these identical classes of persons are alluded to as belonging to Patriarchal society, and no others. These Patriarchs themselves were manifestly independent chiefs of such compound households as we have described. They evidently sought to build up and strengthen their households in the several ways which we have mentioned; and hence, they had in their households servants or subjects corresponding with these several ways.

Abraham, for example, as a wise and courageous chief, had, in his household, all these several classes of persons. 1. He had his own family proper. 2. Others associated with him by mutual agreement, as Lot and his household, for a while. 3. Persons who had been engaged by special contract to unite with his clan, sometimes characterized as "bought with money." 4. And additions by birth within the range of his little kingdom, sometimes called "sons of the house," or "born in the house." These different classes of free persons made up the house of Abraham, the infant Hebrew commonwealth. They belonged to his Patriarchal jurisdiction, and, as such, were his "possession." As subjects thereof, they were, and were often called, "servants." In no case were they ever called *slaves*. Indeed, in all this constitution of the Abrahamic household, there is no place for chattel slavery. Manifestly, these several classes of persons were all free men, women, and children attached to Abraham and his household, *according to the usages and necessities of the times.* Thus, the "bought with money," the "born in the house," and those associated by mutual agreement, were all free fellow-citizens of a Patriarchal nation, in which no trace of chattel slavery is anywhere to be found. Even the words *slave* and *slavery* were unknown and unheard of in the Abrahamic language, so far removed were the things which these words represent, from the great Patriarch's thoughts, practices, and kingdom.

This view of Patriarchal society, and the Patriarchal household, is fundamental to a right understanding of Patriarchal servitude. To illustrate this view, and confirm its correctness, we adduce the following description of a modern chief, and his tribal household, from Dr. W. M. Thomson's "*The Land and the Book.*"

"We encamped for the night near the tent of the Emeer Hussein el 'Fûdle, the supreme chief of all the Arabs in that part of the Jaulan. . . . . We were received with great respect; fresh coffee was roasted, and a sheep brought up, slaughtered, and quickly cooked before our tent, and the extemporaneous feast spread for us in presence of the emeer. Though he did not literally run to the herd and bring it himself, others did, at his bidding, and the whole affair brought the patriarch Abraham vividly to mind. Like our emeer, he dwelt in tents, and his dependents were encamped about him with their flocks and herds. There were not more than thirty tents at this encampment. . . . . They [*i. e.* the people] and their ancestors have belonged to his family for so many generations that all trace of their real origin is lost. . . . . They are the property of the emeer in a restricted sense, and so are the flocks and herds which they are permitted to hold, and he does not hesitate to take what he wants, nor can any refuse his demands, whatever they may be. But then custom, or law, or both, utterly forbids him to sell them. I inquired into all these matters the next day, as we rode through the country, under the protection and guidance of his head-servant, who reminded me constantly of 'Eliezur of Damascus.' In answer to my question, he exclaimed, in indignant surprise, 'Sell us! *istuyfar allah*—God forbid!'"

"They are, in fact, the home-born servants of the very ancient *house* of el Fûdle, and like the 318 in Abraham's family, they are his warriors in time of need, which, in one way or another, happens almost daily. They seem to be attached to the emeer, or rather, perhaps, to his family name, rank, power, and honor. Their own honor, safety, and influence all depend upon him."

In speaking further of the "head-servant" alluded to, Mr. Thomson says that he was "almost startled to find that the emeer was entirely governed by" him. "He [the emeer] does nothing of himself; and this modern Eliezer not only disposes of his master's goods, but manages the affairs of his government very much as he pleases. All the Arabs of the Hûleh and Jaulan greatly fear and court this chief servant."

CHAPTER VII.

SPECIAL FACTS AND CONSIDERATIONS CONFIRMATORY OF THE FOREGOING CONCLUSION THAT CHATTEL SLAVERY HAD NO PLACE IN THE PATRIARCHAL HOUSEHOLDS.

1. POSITIVE evidence of its existence is wholly wanting in the *words and phrases* used to designate and describe the various members of Patriarchal society. If chattel slavery had existed in the Patriarchal households, we should be sure to find it, and

its characteristic facts, designated by terms so definite as to identify it beyond all dispute.   But this is
not the fact.   It is admitted, on all hands, that specific words for *slave* and *slavery* are not found in
ancient Hebrew literature.   It is presumable, to say
the least, that if the thing itself had been there, the
words to represent it would have been there too.

It is, indeed, true, that several words and phrases
appear in the Patriarchal history, which have sometimes been supposed to point to the existence of
chattel slavery.   They are such as the following:
"servant" and "servants," with the corresponding
verb "serve," "men-servants" and "women-serv-
ants," "bondman" and "bondwoman," "bond-servant" and "bondmaid," "maid-servant," "buy" and
"bought with money," "sell" and "sold."

Now, in regard to all these terms, it may be remarked, in general, that Weld, Barnes, Cheever, and
others have abundantly shown that, in themselves,
they have no distinct and specific reference to chattel slavery.

(1.) Their investigations have fully proved that
the distinction which appears in our English translation between "servants" and "bondmen," or "bond-
servants," "maid-servants," and "bondmaids," is
entirely a gloss of the translators.   No such distinction appears in the original Hebrew.   In it the
words are the same, and are used in reference to all
kinds of service and all classes of persons, including
the service of God and the service of the most sacred
friendships, and persons of the highest rank and

character, as Moses, David, Isaiah, and the most distinguished personages of Jewish history. There is not the least intimation, in all the Patriarchal history, that these words ever had a degraded sense; and not one solitary character appears on the arena of ancient Jewish history, who seemed to regard it as dishonorable to apply to himself these identical terms.

(2.) The Hebrew words for "buy" and "sell," and "bought with money," also had a similar general meaning, and had no specific reference to chattel slavery. They were freely applied to cases where chattel slavery was impossible. "Then Joseph said unto the people, Behold I have bought you this day, and your land for Pharaoh."—Gen. xlvii: 23. "Moreover Ruth, the Moabitess, the wife of Mahlon, have I purchased to be my wife."—Ruth iv: 10. In Patriarchal history, the procuring of a wife and the procuring of a servant, are described in the same language. Both were bought with money, were the purchase of silver, the one to be a wife, the other to be a servant, and neither to be a chattel slave.

The truth is, the original Hebrew words for these English terms are such, in their usage, as are perfectly applicable to free men and free society: and such as would have been used if chattel slavery had never been heard of. Therefore they furnish not one particle of positive evidence of the existence of chattel slavery in the Patriarchal households. Indeed, if it had existed there, there would have been another set of words and phrases by which to designate it and its concomitants, and separate it from the free servitude which is described under the terms alluded to above. So that in the absence of specific terms for slavery and its necessary incidents, the terms actually employed indicate that it had no place in Patriarchal society. They are precisely such terms, every one of them, as free Patriarchal society demanded, and not the terms which slaveholding Patriarchal society would have demanded. Later in the history of the world, in other nations, where chattel slavery was superadded to free servitude, we find specific terms to designate it and its concomitants. In the Hebrew language this additional set of terms is wholly wanting.

2. But there is positive evidence in the usage of these terms that the "buying" of servants "with money," as referred to in Patriarchal history, did not and could not mean chattel slavery. The writer of that history, in another Book, has given us, incidentally, a clue to the meaning of this phraseology as found in the Pentateuch, which establishes its sense beyond all question.

Turn, if you please, to Lev. xxv: 47–52, and note the words and phrases there used, and their manifest meaning. The case is that of the poor Jew who should "*sell himself*" to a "stranger or sojourner." He might be redeemed by any of his kindred, or any of his brethren, or he might "*redeem himself*" "*if able.*" "And he shall reckon with him that bought him from the year that he was sold to him unto the year of Jubilee; and the price of his sale shall be according unto the number of years, according to the time of a hired servant shall it be with him."—V. 50. "If there be yet many years behind, according unto them he shall give again the price of his redemption out of the money that he was bought for."—V. 51. Here the servant was "bought with money;" but he also *sold himself:* money was paid for him; but it was paid *to himself*. Most manifestly here is nothing in all this "buying" of the servant "with money," and in his being "sold," but simply an agreement between one free man and another free man, by which the one agrees to perform service for the other, and belong to his household for satisfactory compensation. This is precisely what these terms mean, and all they mean, when used in connection with Abrahamic and Patriarchal history.

In modern times, the buying of negroes with money, means chattel slavery. But this, by no means proves that the buying of servants with money meant chattel slavery in Patriarchal times, where the words *slavery* and *slave* were never heard of. Indeed, the "buying" of servants "with money," can mean chattel slavery only where the existence of chattel slavery has originated and established this specific usage of such language. Everywhere else, such language refers only to bargain between freemen. In free countries, and among free people, such language refers only to engagement for services according to usages of the times. The writer noticed, not long since, among the news items in a secular newspaper printed in Northern Ohio, the following:

"A vagrant in Cincinnati sold her three-days old babe for $3." In Ohio, such language has not the remotest imaginable allusion to chattel slavery : in New Orleans, it would probably refer to nothing else.

So, in Patriarchal times, this sort of phraseology referred simply to the arrangement with the servant himself, to secure his alliance to the household, according to prevailing usages. Chiefs, and heads of families, and clans, could greatly increase their households, and so their strength and influence, by thus enlisting, for money paid *to them*, and not to a third party, such individuals and families as they could induce to join them. This was the Abrahamic and Patriarchal "buying with money." The individuals thus bought were free men, women, and children, who made their own bargain for selling themselves, and did service according to the usages of the times.

3. But this baseless assumption, that Abraham and the Patriarchs bought chattel slaves, by no means warrants the conclusion that they ever held them as such. If we admit that the whole three hundred and eighteen "trained servants" whom Abraham "armed" and led forth to the "slaughter of Chedorlaomer, and of the kings that were with him," were actually bought of somebody after the manner of modern slave-buying, that does not prove at all that Abraham ever thought of making chattel slaves of them himself, or ever held them as such for a single hour.

: Suppose Abraham did buy chattel slaves: did he

ever hold them as such himself? The former supposition throws no light upon the latter question.
To buy a chattel slave out of the hands of a slaveholder, does not constitute the buyer a slaveholder,
by any means. He may be the most ultra abolition-
ist that ever breathed, for all that. If the history
had anywhere said that Abraham did sell, as merchandise, sundry persons, and did actually take money
for them of some third party, and did deliver said
persons over to said third party *as property*, this
would throw great light upon the question whether
he ever held chattel slaves. But this latter sort of
historical evidence happens to be totally wanting.

4. Chattel slavery is a degradation and an oppression so unwelcome and distressful to human beings, that they never did, and never will endure it,
if they can escape from it. In Patriarchal times, all
any slave had to do to escape and be free, was to
use his legs and walk off in full and undisputed possession of that charter of freedom which God Almighty writes upon every human heart while it is
forming in the maternal womb. It was a simple
impossibility for the Patriarchs to hold chattel slaves,
for the very good reason that a single night would
emancipate the whole of them wholly beyond the
power of capture. Nay, they could all walk straight
off at their leisure in broad mid-day sunshine, in
spite of all that the Patriarchs could do to hinder it.
The whole land lay before them, full of game and
fruits, to sustain life : and freedom was just as cheap
to every one of all the servants of the Patriarchs, as

5

slavery. It is the sheerest nonsense to suppose, that, as they journeyed from one part of the country to another, they had a long train of chattel slaves at their heels, like some hideous Legree of our Southern states.

It is said of Abraham, for example, that, at one time, for a certain military expedition, he "armed his servants born in his own house, three hundred and eighteen." If he could muster so many from among his servants that were fit to bear arms, and to be led forth on such an errand, his whole house-hold must have consisted of some thousands. His own household was a sort of traveling kingdom: it existed by itself, separate from all other tribes and households; there was no governmental authority, military force, civil police, or other resource to which he could apply for assistance, outside of the circle of his own tents. How, then, could he hold in the hated subjection of chattel slavery this large number of people? A late eloquent writer has very shrewdly remarked that "the most natural supposi-tion is, that the Patriarch and his wife 'took turns' in surrounding them!"*

5. The necessary concomitants of chattel slavery do not appear in the Patriarchal history. A careful examination of that history does not reveal one soli-tary characteristic of slaveholding society in the Patriarchal households.

(1.) As already noticed, the terms applied to serv-ants have no degraded sense. These terms are so

* Weld.

used as to preclude all idea of degradation. But the idea of great degradation always goes along with chattel slavery; with the word *slave* and the *condition* of a slave. The absence of this in the Patriarchal history, indicates that slavery was not in the Patriarchal families.

(2.) The Patriarchal history does not reveal a chattel slave class of people as distinct and separate from common servants. These two separate classes of people, namely, chattel slaves and common servants, can not be distinguished anywhere in this history. Only one class appears. That class has all the characteristics of common or non-chattel servants. Nowhere does that class present the peculiar characteristics of chattel slaves. But wherever chattel slavery exists, slaves always appear as a class separate and distinct from common or free servants.

(3.) The marketing of servants nowhere appears in the Patriarchal households. There is not in all this history the obscurest hint that the Patriarchs ever sold any of their servants. There is no intimation that they ever regarded them as objects of sale: that the thought of making merchandise of them ever once entered their minds. But who does not know that the selling of slaves always goes along with chattel slavery?

(4.) Nor, again, does the guarding of servants as chattel slaves ever come to light in this history. We never hear a word about the slave-hunt, either with or without blood-hounds, for the capture of the

fugitive.   We hear not one syllable touching Patriarchal valor in reclaiming the guilty runaway: nor ✎
is the snap of the slaveholder's whip, in inflicting
the needed torture upon the quivering flesh, ever
heard.   This whole Patriarchal history is as barren
of all such slaveholding concomitants as the history
of a Connecticut Dorcas Society would be.   The Patriarchs lost, hunted, and sold cattle, and sheep, and
asses, but there is no hint that they ever lost any
slaves, or hunted any, or sold any.   If they never
had any, this is sufficiently accounted for.

(5.) The word *owner* is never applied to masters
in relation to servants.   They were called masters
of the servants under them, but never *owners*.   The
servants are represented in the Patriarchal history
as having been the possession of the master, just as a
man's wife and children are his own, his possession :
but in no instance are they represented as having
been the possession of the master as merchandise.

(6.) The *price* of a man is never the subject of
consideration, while the *wages* are.   Chattel slavery
sets a price upon every slave, and he is known and
estimated by his price.   In free society, the price
of a man is unknown.   Free servants are spoken of
in reference to their wages, and never in reference
to the price of the man himself.

(7.) Neither slave-rebellions, nor the fear of them,
ever appear in the Patriarchal history.   These, and
the fear of them, always go along with chattel slavery.   They mark its entire past history.   In the
nature of things, they must ever belong to it.

6. The characteristics of free society broadly mark this whole history.

(1.) Servants, all the servants there were, constituted an honorable class. No man ever appears to have been dishonored by either being or being called a servant.

(2.) Servants were intrusted with important errands and responsibilities, just as if they were free men, and the official agents of their masters, and in a manner entirely inconsistent with the condition of chattel slaves. It is said of the "eldest servant" of Abraham's house, that he "ruled over all that he had." Of this servant Abraham took an oath, described in the following remarkable language: "Put, I pray thee, thy hand under my thigh: and I will make thee swear by the Lord, the God of heaven, and the God of the earth, *that thou shalt not take a wife unto my son* of the daughters of the Canaanites among whom I dwell. But thou shalt go unto my country, and to my kindred, and take a wife unto my son Isaac."—Gen. xxiv: 2–4. Who ever heard of a chattel slave intrusted with such a responsibility as this in regard to his master's son?

Then the Sacred Record proceeds to tell us that this servant *fitted himself out* for the fulfillment of this sacred promise, with a retinue of "men," and "ten camels," and a large burden of golden "bracelets" and "ear-rings," and "jewels of silver and jewels of gold and raiment," and "precious things." His journey led him across the country, four hundred miles or more, entirely beyond the reach of his master. All this was wholly inconsistent with the existence and necessities of chattel slavery. Other similar events are recorded in the Patriarchal history.

(3.) Servants and masters associated together in a manner consistent only with a state of freedom and manhood equality. Abraham, in the transaction alluded to above, took an oath of his servant, just as if he was his equal. "Swear, I pray thee." And just as if a man's full responsibilities belonged to him. Servants and masters engaged in the same employments together, and dwelt together evidently as equal fellow-citizens, occupying the different relations of servant and master.

(4.) Servants were freely armed and trained for war; armed, trained, and trusted in war, just like loyal citizens, and in circumstances wholly inconsistent with a state of slavery. See the account of Abraham's slaughter of Chedorlaomer, and the kings that were with him. Such arming and training of servants for war, in the circumstances, indicates a state of freedom.

(5.) Servants are the only class of citizens, high or low, alluded to in the Patriarchal history, as belonging to the Patriarchal household. The whole membership, except children, were called servants. Abraham, as well as Isaac, in building up his household, gathered about him many hundreds, and probably thousands of people, and all these are called servants. So of other Patriarchies. The highest, lowest, and only class of citizens known in the Patriarchal history, except children of the chief, are called servants. If all these were chattel slaves, then ancient society consisted of a few score of chiefs, and all the rest of the people were chattel slaves. But this supposition is absurd in the extreme. The servants, therefore, must have been the free fellow-citizens of the Patriarchal kingdom.

(6.) Hence, the fact which distinctly crops out in Patriarchal history, that the servant sometimes became the master's heir. "And Abram said, Behold, to me thou hast given no seed: and, lo, one born in my house is mine heir." If the servants constituted the citizenship of the household, and if the masters were the ruling chiefs of the house, as a little kingdom, this was natural and necessary even, when the chief had no children to whom he could bequeath his authority and place. To build up the house, and transmit it, was a favorite object with the ancients, put into their minds, no doubt, by the Spirit of the Almighty. Of necessity the household must have a head; a head as ruler and guide. It could not exist without such master. Heirship, therefore, fell, of course, to some of the servants, in case the master died childless, inasmuch as servants constituted the membership of the household, and were the only class of people in it. In default of a legitimate heir in the private family of the chief, some member of the general household must become heir to the headship, or the house would be dissolved and scattered.

(7.) Hence, too, the fact that servants acquired, held, and disposed of property as their own, just as if they had all the rights and privileges of free men, and in a manner entirely inconsistent with the existence and necessities of chattel slavery. When Jacob was the servant of Laban, he outstripped his master in the acquisition of property.

(8.) The children of female servants were acknowledged and treated as men and heirs. This chattel slavery forbids. But there is no hint in the Patriarchal history that the children of female servants suffered any degradation on that account. The children of the maid-servants of Leah and Rachel were reckoned among the twelve Patriarchs, precisely in the same manner as were the children of their mistresses. Whoever should say that Ishmael, the son of Hagar, Sarah's handmaid, was a chattel slave, would have a serious account to settle with him, if he were still alive.

Other decisive marks of freedom, as opposed to chattel slavery, might be given, but we forbear. The servitude of the Patriarchal history was either free, non-chattel servitude, more or less restricted, or it was chattel-slave servitude. If it was free servitude, the regulations pertaining to it, and the facts evolved in the history of it, would correspond thereto: if it was slave servitude, the characteristics of slave servitude would appear in the regulations in regard to it, and in the history of it. We have seen that the characteristics of chattel slavery are wholly wanting, and that the marks of free society everywhere abound.

7. Slaveholding is an element of meanness in character which ought not to be charged upon the Patri-

archs unnecessarily. It is a mean thing in any man to regard, or use, or treat his fellow as property.

It is immeasurably more honorable to the Patriarchs to suppose that they gathered about themselves an embryo nation of freemen, and acknowledged fellow citizens, than it is to charge them with the despotism and injustice of reducing the great majority of the membership of their households to the degraded condition of chattel slaves. It was noble in them to do the former: it would have been most ignoble in them if they had been guilty of the latter.

Commentators and expounders of Patriarchal history and character should look well to their proofs, before they set it down as irrefragable orthodoxy, that chattel slaves made up the principal part of the Patriarchal households. Such a stigma upon their character ought not to be admitted without the clearest evidence: such evidence as the Sacred History nowhere gives us.

8. The divine testimony in regard to Abraham and his character utterly forbids the supposition that he himself was a slaveholder, and his servants slaves. God says of him: "For I know him, that he will command his children, and his household after him, and they shall keep the way of the Lord, to do justice and judgment."—Gen. xviii: 19. How perfectly inconsistent this testimony is with the notion that Abraham was the original founder of chattel slavery, the most unjust of all forms of trespass upon manhood rights, and himself the actual leader

and owner of an enormous gang of slaves!   Commentators who suppose this of Abraham, and gravely accuse him of this great wickedness, surely make a most grievous mistake.   God knew Abraham better than this, and has sent down to us a better record of him.   "And they shall keep the way of the Lord to do justice and judgment."

CHAPTER VIII.

PARTICULAR EXAMINATION OF VARIOUS PASSAGES OF SCRIPTURE WHICH REFER TO PATRIARCHAL SERVITUDE.

SEC. 1.—*Noah's Curse.*

IN this investigation we shall not go back beyond the great flood.   It would be useless to attempt to do this.   Howbeit it is a great satisfaction to us who believe in the universal brotherhood of the race, to know that in the first family in the beautiful and holy Garden of Eden, there were no slaves.   God gave Adam a wife to be his companion; but he neither gave to him, nor to Eve his wife, any slaves. There were no slaves in Eden.   There were no slaves in the first family out of Eden.

Passing by the generations before the flood, we begin, then, with the family of Noah, after the flood. And here, too, we have the comfort of knowing that there were no slaves in the Noachian household, unless, indeed, they were overlooked among the cattle and four-footed beasts and creeping things that were crowded into the Ark. Some of the commentators, strangely enough, make Abraham, "the father of the faithful," the actual father and founder of chattel slavery in this world: but the honor of starting the original *idea* has been quite extensively accorded to Noah, in the "*curse*" which it has been supposed he pronounced against Canaan. Whether the great Ark-builder originated the idea himself, or whether he received it as one of the theological achievements of the other side of the flood, or whether it was given to him by divine inspiration, does not very clearly appear. We would respectfully suggest this as an important subject of inquiry for the theological antiquarian. If Noah brought this idea over the flood with him, it is very possible that it may yet be traced back to the very gates of the Garden: or at least to a period coeval with the killing of Abel. It would certainly be interesting to find out that murder and slavery were veritable twin-children of depravity, actually born at the same birth.

But as theological history now runs, chattel slavery was conceived by Noah about the time of his ugly experiment with the wine of the vineyard which he planted, and brought into the world by Abraham, not far from the time when the rite of circumcision was instituted.*   According to this testimony, therefore, its pedigree is of the highest order.

* See Cottage Bible : note, Gen. xvii : 12.

But seriously, the manner in which the Patriarchal prophecy of Noah concerning his sons has been interpreted by certain expounders of Sacred Writ, is a remarkable illustration of the facility with which common sense may be renounced when Bible matters and religious things are the subjects of consideration. It appears, from Bible history, that it was not uncommon, in Patriarchal times, for the aged Patriarch to pronounce a prophetic, farewell benediction upon his children.* This benediction was *prophetic*, and, when inspired, it corresponded with the facts of subsequent history. It changed nothing: it simply spoke, by prophetic foresight, of after facts in the history of the persons concerned. *It, of itself*, really blessed nobody, and it cursed nobody. When, for example, Jacob, thus, in his dying and farewell benediction upon his sons, prophesied in regard to their subsequent history, he did not make one hair white or black as to that history. His prophetic benediction changed nothing: established nothing: decreed nothing. It simply revealed the future, as the spirit of prophecy made that future known to him. It contained in it both good and evil, and, in that sense, both blessing and curse. We call it a *benediction* for the want of a better term, and because it contained in it much more blessing than curse. The old Latin word *dictio*, would, perhaps, be a better word to use in such cases; but usage compels us to retain the word *benediction*, though it properly means only *blessing*.

The history of Noah's life, as given in the book of Genesis, after the account of the flood is closed up at the 17th verse of the ninth chapter, is very brief. It is all contained in the twelve remaining verses of the chapter. These verses contain only three or four incidents of Noah's life after the flood, very briefly described, without any reference, apparently, to the time when they took place, except his death, which is distinctly stated to have occurred *three hundred and fifty years* after the flood. These few incidents took place sometime during these three hundred and fifty years: exactly at what time the Record does not state.

It is altogether probable that Noah planted his vineyard, and became drunken on the wine thereof, not very long after the flood. His unfortunate exposure, as the result of his drinking, and its discovery by his children, must have occurred in immediate connection with his drunkenness. From the Record it appears that Ham, his youngest son, happened to see the nakedness of his father first: of necessity, as the first to notice it, he must have seen it. No one of the sons could have had any knowledge of it at all, except as one of them became an actual eye-witness of it. It so happened that Ham, wittingly or unwittingly, was the first to notice the nakedness of his father. He told his brothers. They, being thus informed of the matter, had no need to witness their father's degradation, and so they "took a garment" "and went backward and covered the nakedness of their father." Whether Ham, or either of the other sons, was at all to blame in all this, doth not appear from the Sacred Record. The presumption, is that none of the children were to blame. Blame, doubt-

less, attached to the father.   He awoke from his
wine, and had the chagrin to know that his younger
son had been an eye-witness of his degradation, and
that all his sons were thus made acquainted with it.

The rest of Noah's life after the flood, of three
hundred and fifty years, is passed over in silence,
except his farewell, prophetic benediction upon his
sons.   This is recorded in the 25th, 26th, and 27th
verses of this ninth chapter.   It is not said *when* this
was uttered: but, from the nature of the utterance
itself, and from the circumstances of the case, it is
altogether probable, nay, morally certain, that this
prophecy was uttered near the close of his life.   It
was a dying, farewell *dictio* respecting his sons, as to
their after history: it is the last thing said of the
venerable Patriarch, next to the account of his death:
near the close of his life was the most suitable time
for such an utterance.   We protest most fully against
the notion that such a solemn, inspired prophecy as
this, was uttered by Noah just as he was coming out
of a drunken fit!   What witless and morbid stupidity
has possessed commentators to favor such an absurd
idea, is more than we can comprehend.   As if drunkenness was favorable for the reception of the Holy
Spirit for the gift of prophecy!

In this farewell utterance of Noah respecting the
future of his sons, not one word is said of Ham,
either good or evil, except that which is spoken of
Canaan his son.   There were very good reasons for
referring especially to Canaan.   The most prominent
thing in regard to Ham, before the mind of the dy-

ing Patriarch, was the miserable future of his son Canaan. This was especially and strongly presented before his mind, by the spirit of prophecy, undoubtedly because the Canaanites would be so closely connected with subsequent manifestations of Jehovah to the world. They were to be the objects of special divine judgments for their iniquities, to be executed, in part, by God's chosen people. This is reason enough why they should be particularly referred to by the dying Patriarch. But, in speaking of this miserable future of the son of Ham, Noah really makes no curse: decrees nothing: entails nothing either upon Ham or upon Canaan: he simply reveals beforehand what was to be the future. That future was a miserable, cursed future: but Noah did not make it so by any thing he said. Prophecy does not make the future of which it speaks: it only reveals it beforehand.

This prophetic utterance of the dying Patriarch has no connection whatever with Ham's accidental, and for aught the Record states, innocent notice of his father's shame. It was probably spoken hundreds of years after that incident occurred.* That people, and even grave commentators, can so far lose their wits as to imagine that Noah, just as he was coming out of a fit of intoxication, was inspired by Almighty God to pronounce a terrible malediction,

---

* It is no very unusual thing in Scripture for events, and even centuries, to be dropped out between two consecutive verses, and those linked together as if in immediate succession, which, in fact, were widely separated."—PROF. E. HITCHCOCK, D. D.

as a divine judgment upon Canaan and his children, for the assumed wickedness of Ham, his father, is certainly a great marvel. This is making the children's teeth snap for the iniquities of the father, in right good earnest. And then, to extend this supposed malediction to the other children of Ham, and their descendants, concerning whom nothing at all is said in the Sacred Record, and make that a warrant for enslaving said descendants, and committing all sorts of wrong upon them, puts the worst logic the devil ever used altogether in the background. Brave, indeed, are they that can swallow such doctrines and interpretations, and believe them precious morsels of divine inspiration!

"Cursed be Canaan; a servant of servants shall he be unto his brethren." This prophecy concerning Canaan, which was not otherwise a prophecy concerning Ham, and which had nothing to do with the other children of Ham, and hence nothing to do with the Africans, received its fulfillment in the after history of the Canaanites. The prophetic curse was uttered *against* Canaan, and it was fulfilled *upon* Canaan, that is, upon his descendants. It has, therefore, no more to do with the inhabitants of Africa, than it has with the serfs of Russia, the people of Ireland, or the American Indians; and if it had, it would no more justify the enslavers of the Africans, than our Savior's prediction that Judas should betray him justified the traitor in the murderous betrayal of his Master. Prophecy of future wickedness furnishes no justification for its perpetration.

It even adds guilt to such perpetration, by carrying with it some sort of warning against it.

Sec. 2.—*Hagar.*

" Now Sarai, Abram's wife, bore him no children : and she had a handmaid, an Egyptian, whose name was Hagar."—Gen. xvi : 1. "Had" her how ? as a *slave*, or as a *handmaid?* The Record says, as "a handmaid." She is nowhere called a *slave*, and there is not the least hint, in the whole Mosaic account of her, that she was a slave. The history which we have of her in the book of Genesis, clearly shows that she occupied, in the Abrahamic household, the first place, on the female side, next to Sarah : as Eliezer of Damascus occupied the first place next to Abraham, on the male side. To count either of these persons as slaves, totally mistakes the constitution of the Abrahamic household ; and is as wide of the mark as it would be to pronounce the venerable Secretary of State, of the late administration, and the lady who presided at the White House in Washington, President Buchanan's *slaves* : every whit as far from the truth. Abraham was a prince, at the head of a powerful clan : Sarah, his wife, was a princess, as her name signifies : the persons on both sides nearest to them, and most intimately associated with them, were Eliezer and Hagar : Eliezer as steward, or first overseer of affairs, and Hagar as the handmaid, or maid of honor, to Sarah. Eliezer was of Damascus, and Hagar was of Egypt— foreigners of the most honorable type. They were both, as connected with the Abrahamic household, or

6

nation, the subjects of Abraham: and hence, in accordance with the common language of the times,
they were called *servants*. The *official servants* of a
leading prince or chief are a long way from being
chattel slaves. Eliezer and Hagar are never called
slaves: and there is not the least intimation in the
Sacred History that they ever occupied the position
of slaves. A brief survey of the history of Hagar
will show that she was far enough from occupying
the position of a chattel slave.

Sarah, finding herself barren, and despairing of
seeing the promise fulfilled of a numerous seed, undertook to remedy the difficulty, according to the
custom of the princes of the times, by seeking to
obtain children by her Egyptian handmaid. This
may appear to us moderns, now that the earth is
crowded with people, and infanticide common, and
barrenness is regarded as a favor rather than otherwise, as a very foolish procedure. But in order to
understand it fully, we need to remember, that, in
the early ages, the desire of a numerous offspring
was one of the strongest sentiments pervading the
minds of the people. As a public sentiment, the
desire of perpetuating name and family was over-
whelming. In modern times, even, this sentiment
sometimes becomes very strong. Under its influence the great Napoleon committed the same mistake which Sarah, the princess of Abraham, did, and
upon that mistake dashed his fortunes to fragments.
Sarah was determined to remedy the calamity and
disgrace of her barrenness, to have the promise ful-

filled, and to secure seed, and the perpetuity of the family. Abraham was carried away with the plan, though it is manifest that he was afterward sorely rebuked by the Almighty for his weakness and unbelief. So Sarah "took Hagar, her maid, the Egyptian, and gave her to her husband Abram, to be his wife." Hagar is called "the Egyptian," as denoting her origin, not by way of reproach, but by way of honor. Egypt was then the most powerful and honorable nation in the world, and to be an Egyptian, at that time, was a most honorable distinction, much as it was afterward to be a Roman, when Rome came to be in the ascendant. And Hagar, the high-born and proud Egyptian, maid of honor to the princess Sarah, became Abraham's wife, and she bare him a son. Now, abating the first mistake, this was an honorable transaction. Its object was to secure heirship in the family. But it is morally certain that Sarah, the princess, would never have given to Abraham, her lord, a mighty prince of the land, a *slave* for such a purpose as this; and that Abraham would never have accepted of a *mere slave* for such a purpose. It is infinitely absurd to suppose this. The first mistake being granted and remembered, it is absolutely certain that Sarah would select for Abraham the lady highest in honor, and esteem, and rank in the household. Hence she gave him "to be his wife"—to occupy, for the time being, the same place in relation to Abraham which she herself, a princess, occupied, not a *slave*, but her own chosen handmaid, Hagar, of the rich and noble Egyptian

stock. The object was to secure honorable heirship
in the family. How absurd to suppose, that in the
household of a mighty prince, a *slave* would be selected for such a purpose!

But when the honor of being the mother of the
Abrahamic nation appeared likely to be transferred
from the true princess and wife, to Hagar, Sarah
began to see her mistake. To secure this honor for
herself, was the object of this maneuver; but when
the thing was done, Sarah's eyes were opened to see
how the matter would eventuate, and that this plan
would really supplant herself, and make Hagar the
princess and mother of Israel. She appealed to Abraham for redress. But after things had proceeded
thus far, what could he do by way of redress? His
reply, however, is magnanimous, and fully exhonor-
ates him from all base and ignoble desires in this
whole affair. "Behold thy maid is in thy hand; do
to her as it pleaseth thee." 'The plan was yours
from the outset; at your request I yielded to it, and
only as far as you desired; you can do what you
choose with Hagar; it was great folly in us both;
whatever you can do to repair the mischief, you are
at full liberty to do; I have no claim upon Hagar,
and do not wish to have any; the Lord Jehovah for-
give this our unbelief and foolishness!' Sarah, the
prime agent in this wickedness, chagrined and pro-
voked, sought relief, human-nature-like, by trying
to degrade Hagar. She bore the abuse of her queenly
mistress as long as she well could, and then, just
exactly when it pleased her, she left Abraham's house-

hold, to take care of herself. She, doubtless, had had her share in the wickedness involved in this unhappy affair, and so it was fit that she should have some share in the mischiefs resulting. But let it evermore be remembered that Hagar left her adopted household a free woman, just when she pleased, and went whithersoever she would; and it does not appear that there was any slave-hunt to catch her, or bring her back.

This piece of wickedness, the result of a mistaken notion at the outset, was a terrible blow to the happiness of the Patriarch's family. But after the thing was done, it could not be undone or altered. The only question then was, What could be done to remedy it? God had far-reaching purposes concerning this son of Abraham, by Hagar, though he was by no means the true heir. Hence the angel of the Lord, that met her in the wilderness, directed her to return to Abraham's household, and if she returned, of course, she must acknowledge Sarah as first princess in the family, and submit to her authority as superior. As a female member of the household, she must be subject to her; she must "submit herself under her hands." Although her position had been a high and honorable one, nevertheless, she must be subject to the female head of the clan. In all this, there is not the least intimation that she was to be put into, or occupy, the place of a slave. So Hagar, of genuine Egyptian blood, became the mother of that wonderful race, the Ishmaelites, next in honor and rank in the Abrahamic family, to Sarah, the true princess, and mother of that still more wonderful people, the Jews, from whom, as concerning the flesh, our Lord and Savior sprang.

NOTE.—Effort is sometimes made to convict Abraham and Sarah of slaveholding, in the case of Hagar on the ground of what the apostle Paul says of Hagar, as a "bondwoman," in the Epistle to the Galatians. Our English translation makes him call her a "bondwoman." But this is not calling her a "*slave*." He might have contemplated her as a "bondwoman," in a variety of senses, without regarding her at all as a *slave bondwoman*. Indeed, a little careful examination shows, at once, that Paul regarded Hagar as in some particular sense a "bondwoman," as she was, but not at all as a "*slave bondwoman*," as she was not. The Greek word which he applies to her, and which is translated "*bondwoman*," is never used elsewhere in the New Testament to mean a *slave*, or any thing like it. That word is παιδίσκη, *paidiskee*, and properly means *a girl*, or *young maiden*. This word occurs only in seven other passages in the New Testament; to all of which we will refer, in order that the reader may see for himself what the usage is. Matt. xxvi: 69—"Now Peter sat without in the palace: and a '*damsel*' came unto him, saying, Thou also wast with Jesus of Galilee." Mark xiv: 66, 69—"And as Peter was beneath in the palace, there cometh one of the '*maids*' of the high priest." "And a '*maid*' saw him again," etc. Luke xiv; 45

—" And shall begin to beat the men-servants and
'*maidens*,'" etc. xxii: 56—"But a certain '*maid*'
beheld him [Peter] as he sat by the fire," etc.
John xviii: 17 — "Then saith the '*damsel*' that
kept the door unto Peter," etc. Acts xii: 13—"A
'*damsel*' came to hearken named Rhoda," etc. xvi:
16—" And it came to pass, as we went to prayer, a
certain '*damsel*' possessed with a spirit of divination
met us," etc.

These passages embrace all the places in the New
Testament where the word which Paul applies to
Hagar in Galatians, and which is translated "bondwoman," occurs. If the reader will bear in mind
the fact, stated by Kitto, that slavery did not exist
in the land of Judah at the time the events alluded
to in these passages took place, he will see, at once,
that there is not, in any of them, the remotest possible
allusion to *slave* or *slavery*. In a land of freedom
'*damsel*' does not mean *slave*. The Septuagint translation of the Old Testament applies this same word
to Ruth, in the Book of Ruth, iv: 12, who, surely,
was not a *slave*, though Boaz does say he "purchased" her; not, indeed, to be his *slave*, but "*to be
his wife!*" There is, therefore, not the least shadow of evidence that Paul had the most distant
reference to *slave* or *slavery* in what he says of
Hagar in his Epistle to the Galatians. And besides
this testimony from the usage of words, we are to
remember that no Jew, as we have already seen, would
ever think of regarding the mother of Ishmael as a
slave, much less such a Hebrew writer as was Saint

Paul. The *idea* of slave was an exotic in the ancient Hebrew mind, never sufficiently naturalized to it to have a Hebrew word to express it. It is a gross and total mistake to be looking for slavery at every crook and turn of Bible language. Its writers all wrote under the light and liberty of freedom. Slavery was a thing almost wholly unknown to them. They were unacquainted with it : they were not familiar with it. The apostle Paul uses language, as do all the writers of the Bible, not in the base South Carolina sense, but in the ancient, free, Hebrew sense.

SEC. 3.—*Gen.* xvii : 12–27.

Verse 12. "And he that is eight days old shall be circumcised among you, every man-child in your generations, he that is born in the house, or bought with money of any stranger which is not of thy seed." This verse is found in the middle of the history of the institution of the rite of circumcision. We beg leave to quote the passage entire, from the 9th verse to the 14th inclusive :

"9. And God said unto Abraham, Thou shalt keep my covenant therefore, thou, and thy seed after thee, in their generations.

"10. This *is* my covenant, which ye shall keep, between me and you, and thy seed after thee; Every man-child among you shall be circumcised.

"11. And ye shall circumcise the flesh of your foreskin; and it shall be a token of the covenant betwixt me and you.

"12. And he that is eight days old shall be circumcised among you, every man-child in your generations; he that is born in the house, or bought with money of any stranger, which *is* not of thy seed.

"13. He that is born in thy house, and he that is bought with thy money, must needs be circumcised: and my covenant shall be in your flesh for an everlasting covenant.

"14. And the uncircumcised man-child, whose flesh of his foreskin is not circumcised, that soul shall be cut off from his people; he hath broken my covenant."

This is the Mosaic account of the institution of the rite of circumcision. The rite itself is only a "token," sign, or seal of a "covenant."

One of the fundamental characteristics of this rite was, that it should include *every male* in the Abrahamic household. In making the rite universal, without exception as to the males in the Abrahamic household, allusion is distinctly made, in the 12th and 13th verses, to the *different elements* of that household. Three distinct classes of persons are designated, as embracing the whole circle of the household; namely, (1,) the children proper; (2,) children "born in the house," not of the family proper; (3,) and those bought with money, which were of foreign blood. These three classes of persons belonged to the Patriarchal household, and were members of it; hence they are distinctly designated in this account of the institution of the rite of circumcision. The language here used was not designed to describe particularly the social *status*, or condition of these several classes; but rather to refer to them as existing classes, all of which were to be included in the rite of circumcision. The object of the writer, in

7

referring to these several classes, manifestly was, simply to include *all* the elements of the Patriarchal household in the rite of circumcision. The phrase, "bought with money," or more accurately, "the purchase of silver," designates, with sufficient clearness, one class of persons belonging to the household, but determines nothing, as we have seen, in regard to the social condition of those so bought. Free servants could be "the purchase of silver" just as well as slave servants. For we learn from other sources, that this phrase, "bought with money," commonly referred to *services*, and not to *persons*, in the sense of property, at all; and hence the presumption always is, when this phrase is used in regard to servants, that it refers to free servants, whose services have been bought of themselves.

The peculiar phraseology of our translation of the 12th verse of this seventeenth chapter of Genesis, is liable to an erroneous interpretation. The phrase, "bought with money of any stranger, which is not of thy seed," may be understood as referring to persons bought of others, a third party, who were the sellers. But this is manifestly not the meaning of the original Hebrew. The true meaning is that given by Prof. Bush, in his translation of this passage, which is as follows: "A son of eight days old shall be circumcised unto you; every male in your generations, the born in the house, and the purchase of silver, from, that is, even or including every son of the stranger, which is not of thy seed." On this passage he also remarks: "This passage affords no countenance to the idea of Abraham's having bought slaves of others who claimed an ownership in them." The idea of a third party, of whom the individuals referred to were bought, does not belong to the passage at all. Prof. J. Morgan, D. D., of Oberlin College, Ohio, gives the following translation of this same verse: "He that is eight days old shall be circumcised among you, every male of your generations, the house-born and the money-purchase of any stranger, who is not of thy seed." In regard to the phrase, "of any stranger," he remarks, that it "denotes the *origin* or *source* of the purchased servant, but does not determine the seller, who, for aught this expression certainly shows, might be the purchased one himself." Other authorities and opinions might be given to the same effect. The commentary habit of making this passage teach that Abraham had *chattel slaves*, is sheer mistake foisted upon God's pure Bible out of that enormous pro-slavery sink, modern pro-slavery prejudice. This passage of Scripture only innocently refers to the different elements which entered into the Patriarchal household, for the purpose of making the rite of circumcision include the whole, without exception. Of precisely the same import is the 27th verse of this same chapter, a literal translation of which is as follows: "And all the men of his house, the home-born, and the purchase of money from with the stranger, were circumcised with him."

These passages are interesting as giving us a clue to the constitution and several elements of the Pa-

triarchal household. This constitution, as we have
seen, grew out of the nature of the case, and the
necessities of the times. These elements were the
natural and necessary elements of the compound Patriarchal family. These elements, as we have before
proved, were, of necessity, free elements, attached to
the household in different ways, according to well
understood and universal usages. They have no
more to do with chattel slavery than they have to
do with Indian pow-wows. To make slavery out of
any of these elements is a simple gratuity, hatched in
modern theological ovens, and made to peep to pacify
the consciences of modern slaveholding criminals.

Sec. 4.—*Joseph.*

According to the current interpretation of the Old
Testament Scriptures, Joseph must surely have been
a *slave.* To doubt this, lays one open to suspicions
of irreverence for the Bible, if not of downright infidelity. And here we make our confession. We
believe most fully that God has given to the world
a veritable Bible : that that Bible has been preserved
to and for the race : that the writings now known as
the Hebrew and Greek Scriptures are that Bible : and
we believe, moreover, that, according to this genuine
Bible, Joseph, eleventh son of Jacob, true son of
Isaac, promised son of Abraham, never was in the
condition of a chattel slave, the current notion to the
contrary notwithstanding. We believe that a careful and candid examination of the true Scripture

account of Joseph, as given in the Book of Genesis, and alluded to elsewhere in the Bible, will show that Joseph was never considered as a slave either by those whom he served, or by himself. Our object in seeking to make this appear, is not so much to vindicate the Bible from pro-slavery interpretations, as to throw additional light upon the constitution of Patriarchal and primitive society, as being a state of society free from chattel slavery, and as having, in its stead, various forms of *free servitude*. Right at this point lies the great mistake that has been made in the interpretation of the Old Testament Scriptures on the subject of slavery. Ignorance of the constitution and genius of Patriarchal and primitive society has converted ancient free servitude into modern chattel slavery, and so has foisted a monstrous and abominable perversion upon the Sacred Record, which absolutely threatens its utter subversion.

But if we admit that Joseph was really a slave, and was so held and treated, the pro-slavery side of the question gains nothing, inasmuch as the divine disapprobation is clearly expressed against all the oppressive treatment which Joseph received at the hand of his brethren and others. It is not, therefore, to vindicate the history of Joseph from pro-slavery abuse, which, after all, is but a harmless abuse, that we enter upon its examination, but rather, if possible, to set that history in its true light, as a help to a right understanding of the social status of the times.

"Now, Israel loved Joseph more than all his children, because he was the son of his old age:" but
his brethren "envied" him and "hated" him.—
Gen. xxxvii. When, therefore, their father Jacob
sent Joseph to his brethren in Dotham, to see whether
it was well with them and the flocks, they conspired
against him and sought to kill him. The result of
their conspiracy, however, was, that he was "sold"
to the Ishmaelites, and by them taken down into
Egypt and "sold" to "Potiphar, an officer of Pharaoh's, and captain of the guard." Most persons
who read this account, suppose, as a matter of course,
that if Joseph was "sold" by one party, and "bought"
by another, he was sold as a chattel slave, and bought
as a chattel slave. They suppose this, because this
is the modern sense of buying and selling, when applied to persons. But this is purely a pro-slavery
mistake. The fact of *buying and selling*, in ancient
usages, proves nothing in regard to *the condition
into which the individuals were bought.* Anciently,
fathers "sold" their daughters to their intended
husbands, for money: and men "bought" their intended wives, and paid money for them. But the
fathers sold their daughters not into the condition
of chattel slaves, but into the condition of *wives:*
and the husbands bought their wives not into the
condition of chattel slaves, but into the condition of
wives: and the whole transaction had no more to do
with chattel slavery, than it had with the man in the
moon. In those times, "buying" and "selling"
did not mean slavery, as now. In the early settle-

ment of Virginia, the settlers being destitute of wives, English merchantmen brought over cargoes of young women from the mother country and sold them to the needy settlers for one hundred and twenty pounds of tobacco apiece. Sold them for what? Slaves? No: *for wives*. The buying and selling did not make them slaves. It only very innocently made them genuine wives—that is all. The buying and selling did not determine the condition or state into which they were bought. So the buying and selling of Joseph determines nothing in regard to the condition into which he was bought.

It is manifest that Joseph was sold by his brethren, not as a chattel slave, but as a hated and disagreeable member of the household, of whom they wished to be rid. Their object was to get rid of him, as an annoyance. At first, they proposed to kill him; and, undoubtedly, would have killed him, if the special providence of God had not presented before them another method of getting him out of the way. Joseph was, doubtless, well aware of their intentions, and, in all probability, expressly consented to the disposition that was afterward made of him. Perhaps it was at his earnest solicitation, seconded by that of Judah, that they determined to shuffle him off to the Ishmaelites, who, being on their way to Egypt, would be likely to take him fully out of the way. Of course, if they could get a few pieces of silver in making the transfer, they would do it. They thus shuffled him off from the family, not as their slave, but as a troublesome member. There is not the remotest shadow of evidence that the brethren of Joseph either regarded or sold him as a slave. They simply wished to get rid of him, to get him out of the household. So they thrust him out, and delivered him into the hands of an Ishmaelitish tribe, or caravan, who were traveling to Egypt. They were "merchantmen:" but not slave-traders, any more than the English merchantmen who carried the English ladies to Virginia, and sold them for a hundred and twenty pounds of tobacco apiece, were slave-traders. There is not the most distant intimation in the Sacred History that these Ishmaelites were merchantmen in slaves. They were merchantmen, traveling to Egypt, but not slave-dealers.

The lad Joseph being thus forcibly thrust out, and forbidden to return on peril of his life, and being under the necessity of being somewhere connected with some household or tribe, or of being a solitary, wandering vagabond, and being forcibly delivered over, and transferred to the Ishmaelites, had no alternative but to go with them and be their servant: that is, belong to the company, or clan, as a bought-with-money servant. This forcible transfer did not make him a chattel slave. I have seen lads of much the same age, in free, Puritan New England, forcibly transferred from one family to another, and nobody ever dreamed of slavery in the case. The Ishmaelites manifestly received Joseph as a bought-with-money servant: an unchattelized servant of that class, and by no means as a chattel slave. As such, they made a transfer of him for money to Potiphar.

chief marshal of Egypt. That he was so received by
the Egyptian officer is manifest from the subsequent
history. The Mosaic account proceeds to say, that
"The Lord was with Joseph," in the house of his
master, and "he was a *prosperous man.*" Not a
good slave, but a "*prosperous man.*" The whole
record assumes that Joseph considered himself, and
was recognized by others, as occupying the position
of a free serving man, and not that of a slave. As
a free serving man, he very speedly arose to the position of chief officer in the household of his master.
Note the language: "And Joseph found grace in his
sight, and he served him." "*Served*" him when?
At the very time when he was highest in the confidence and favor of his master. At the hight of his
prosperity in the house of his master he still "*served.*"
Served how? as a slave? By no means: but as first
officer and manager of all that he had! So the Record
reads. Now this is never the course of affairs where
the condition of things is that of chattel slavery.
No slave bought with money, after the modern
Southern method of buying, and in the Southern
sense, could ever rise to be first officer in the household of Major-Gen. Scott. Potiphar was chief marshal of the kingdom: Joseph was first officer and
overseer in his house. This is not the history of a
chattel slave. It never can be. It is the history of
a recognized free man, attached to the house of Potiphar, precisely in accordance with the custom of the
times; at first, indeed, as a bought-with-money servant, but always as a goodly and prosperous man.

And when Potiphar's wife accused Joseph falsely before his master, and his wrath was kindled against Joseph, Potiphar proceeds against him and punishes him altogether as a recognized man, and not as a degraded, chattel slave. Joseph is not whipped and sent back to his slave task; he is not sold off from the premises; but he is put into the prison "where the king's prisoners were bound:" all as an unchattelized man—as an official character guilty of crime, and not at all as a chattel slave.

. So, during all the time in which he was a prisoner, he appears as an unchattelized man-prisoner, and, in no respect, as a slave-prisoner. Joseph's history in prison is manifestly the history of a recognized free man; forcibly thrust away, indeed, from his native household and nation, and attached to a foreign family in a foreign land. It is a history impossible to a chattel slave. Notice Joseph's request to the chief butler: "But think on me when it shall be well with thee, and show kindness, I pray thee, unto me, and make mention of me unto Pharaoh, and bring me out of this house." And make mention of me unto Pharaoh! What a request for a mere chattel slave, of foreign and hated blood, thrown into prison by the chief marshal of the kingdom, for asserted, flagrant crime, to present to a high officer of the most powerful monarch that then pressed an earthly throne! What had a miserable slave, in an Egyptian dungeon, to do with an Egyptian Pharaoh, in the days of Egyptian greatness and splendor? Who ever heard of such a request as this from the jails or slave-pens of Washington finding its way up into the White House? The truth is, this is history that never belongs to slavery, and such as can belong only to freedom. If Joseph had been the slave property of Potiphar, he would have had more sense than to have made such a request as this : just as there is not a slave in all the South who has not more sense than to present such a request as this to any President of the United States.

Well, time passes on, and Pharaoh has a remarkable dream. They send for Joseph to interpret it. In all the history that follows, there is not the least intimation or indication that Joseph was regarded as occupying the condition of a slave. Let him who doubts this statement find it, if he can. But meanwhile, observe one or two incidental particulars. "And it came to pass, at the end of *two full years*, that Pharaoh dreamed." Joseph, then, had been confined in the prison *two full years*, Did Potiphar lose these *two full years* of slave service? Or did the royal treasury open its coffers, and grant him remuneration? Or what did poor Potiphar do about these *two full years* of slave service due him? The history certainly leaves us in great darkness and trouble concerning Potiphar's pay. It does not even say one word about this slaveholder's whining over his loss. Strange that he did not think to tie up this Hebrew dog, and give him a sound flogging, and send him back to his work again, and so save these *two full years* of slave labor. A blundering fellow he, for chief marshal of mighty Egypt, and strangely destitute of modern wit.

"Then Pharaoh sent and called Joseph, and they brought him hastily out of the dungeon: and he shaved himself and changed his raiment and came in unto Pharaoh." Indeed! What business had this piece of Potiphar's property with the toilet and changes of raiment? What odds does it make with the miserable slave how he appears before the great ones of earth? and where did Joseph get his changes of raiment? Were there abolitionists in Egypt in those days to make the needed contribution? Or did master slaveholding Potiphar expect a big, round sum for this job of dream-interpretation, and so rigged Joe out in court-style, especially for the occasion? When a similar affair is got up at the "White House," "may I be there to see!"

We beseech the reader to turn to the forty-first chapter of Genesis, and read carefully the whole chapter through, with this one inquiry in his mind: "Is this the history of a chattel slave, or is it the history of a free man?" Stop, we pray thee, right here, and get your Bible and read the whole chapter, and we are sure that you will be ready to say with us, that such history as this never did and never can belong to slavery. Do not say that Joseph *must* have been a slave after all. There is no "must" about it, except what modern pro-slavery prejudice has affixed to the case. A careful examination of the history, in the light of the social arrangements of

society in those early times, before oppression and
trespass upon personal rights had extended to chat-
telism, shows at once that slavery was not there.
And if American slavery should exist ten thousand
years, we should have neither fear, nor hope, that
such a piece of history as this would ever turn up.
There is not the least evidence in all the history of
Joseph, that he was ever treated or regarded in
Egypt as a chattel slave. His interview with Pharaoh has all the characteristics of an interview of a
free man with a monarch acknowledging him as
such. His bearing is noble, manly, and dignified.
Base slavery is not there. If it had been, the king's
ring had never been put upon Joseph's hand, the
golden chain had never been put about his neck,
and the royal vestures had never clothed his goodly
person. Slavery would have sent him sneaking off
to his kennel and to his pack-horse service, to wear
his life out in dehumanizing work, and subserviency
to the robber-will of another, without pay.

NOTE.—In the 105th Psalm, commencing at the
17th verse, occurs the following passage: "He sent
a man before them, even Joseph, who was sold for a
servant: Whose feet they hurt with fetters: he was
laid in iron: Until the time that his word came:
the word of the Lord tried him. The king sent and
loosed him: even the ruler of the people, and let
him go free. He made him lord of his house, and
ruler of his substance: To bind his princes at his
pleasure: and teach his senators wisdom."

" Who was sold for a servant." Some of the commentators say he was sold for a slave. But this
passage does not say that : nor is that said anywhere
in the Bible. This Psalm says he was sold for a
servant: whether for a slave servant, or for a free
servant, it does not specify. It is great hermeneutical blundering to give a specific and limited sense
to a general term when there is nothing in the connection to demand it. Even if Joseph was a *slave,*
there is no authority for making this Psalm say so :
for it does not say so, any more than the Sacred
Record says that Moses, and David, and Paul, were
slaves. It says truly, that Joseph was sold for a
servant, but what kind of a servant, it does not say.
It is only by assuming that Joseph *was* a slave, that
the commentators make this passage from the Psalms
call Joseph a slave. The passage itself says no such
thing. You might just as well assume that Joseph
was a porter-servant in some ancient Egyptian hotel,
and translate : " He was sold for a porter ;" or that
he was a sexton-servant, and translate : " He was
sold for a sexton ;" as to assume that he was a slaveservant, and translate : " He was sold for a slave."

" Whose feet they hurt with fetters : he was laid
in iron : Until the time that his word came : the
word of the Lord tried him." All this refers unquestionably to the time when he was in prison :
and hence has nothing to do with his condition as a
servant, whether he was a slave or not. " Whose
feet *they* hurt with fetters." Not Potiphar, his master, as a slaveholder, but, as Dr. Alexander explains :

"the Egyptians, or his gaolers." The king sent and loosed him: even the ruler of the people, and let him go free." In regard to this verse, Dr. Alexander also says: "Both verbs strictly apply to the removal of his fetters, the first meaning properly to knock off, the other to open for the purpose of removing." The sense, then, of this, is simply that the king, Pharaoh, having doubtless become satisfied of Joseph's innocence, brought him out of prison. There is not the least imaginable allusion to emancipating him as a slave. An infinitely shallow place this, to fish for Bible slavery.

These verses allude to Joseph just as if he was a free man, and not at all as if he was a slave. They refer to the fact that he was sold for a servant, that he was imprisoned and fettered, and lay there for the trial of his faith till the king sent and brought him out; and that Pharaoh placed him next to the throne as lord of his house and ruler of Egypt: all just as if Joseph was, all the while, a free man, and not at all as if he was a slave. And if our minds had not become accustomed to pro-slavery ideas and practices, and debauched with pro-slavery interpretations of the Word of God, we should no more think of looking for slavery in such passages of Scripture as this, than we should in the valediction at the end of Wilberforce's letters: "Your obedient *servant.*" It would be a great deliverance indeed, if the American mind could be relieved of the illusion that *servant* means *slave.* This would let great light into a very dark place.

CHAPTER IX.

A WONDERFUL AND SUBLIME PROPHECY

" For I know him, that he will command his children and his household after him, and they shall keep the way of the Lord to do justice and judgment; that the Lord may bring upon Abraham that which he hath spoken of him."—Gen. xviii: 19.

THIS is the word of the Lord, concerning Abraham. It is both testimony to present fact, and prophecy in regard to the future.

It seems to have been the divine arrangement in populating the earth after the flood, that particular individuals should be representative fathers of families, tribes, peoples, and nations. Such individuals were endowed with the power of national progeniture. As type progenitors, they gave cast and character to the whole line of their posterity. Canaan begat Canaanites—children after his own likeness. Ishmael had Ishmaelites for sons and daughters in all after time. So of other representative and type men of antiquity. They were fathers and founders of races, carrying their own image and superscription to all generations.

To this class of venerable ancients, Abraham belonged. He was the father and founder of a peculiar and wonderful people. His children, the Jews, can not be mistaken. They are still, always have been, and, doubtless, always will be, strongly Abrahamic. Without controversy, they all have Abraham for their father. And notwithstanding the present dispersion and national degradation of the Jews, it must be confessed that Abraham, their great father, stands apart from all the rest of the national patriarchs of antiquity, as the noblest specimen of a type-progenitor and nation-founder of which the nations can boast. His name, as connected with the world's history, is more sacred and venerable than that of any other ancient Patriarch known to us.

Now, the grand characteristic which distinguishes him above all other national patriarchs of the ancient times, is that which is contained in the remarkable declaration concerning him, quoted at the head of this chapter. This characteristic embraced in it two fundamental particulars: (1,) True obedience to God as supreme; and (2,) True judgment and justice toward man. "And they shall keep the way of the Lord to do justice and judgment." These were fundamental elements in Abraham's character, distinguishing and exalting him above all other nation-builders of antiquity. On the basis of these elements, he established his household. The members thereof, with himself at the head, kept "the way of the Lord," and did justice and judgment.

The true righteousness of obedience to the Lord Jehovah of hosts, and of upright judgment and justice to man, *was the Abrahamic peculiarity*, and by

8

it he, as ancestral head, and his posterity after him,
were to be distinguished from all other families and
nations.   True Jehovah worship and love, and true
man worship and love, were thus to be, from the
beginning, the peculiarity of the Abrahamic race.
This was the element of separation, this the mark
of distinction, this the type of character which distinguished the great Patriarch himself, and which
was to descend in the line of his posterity, and ultimately, by spiritual succession, to reach all the families of the earth.

Abraham's Jehovah worship was the true religion,
testified to as such by both Jesus Christ and his
Apostles.   Abraham's "justice to man" was the true
philanthropy, including all proper liberty to all, and
excluding all oppression, and all wrong.   Thus RE-
LIGION and LIBERTY constituted the Abrahamic bap-
tism, the Abrahamic mark of separation, the national
characteristic of the Abrahamic stock.

If, now, from the point in the history of the ages
where we stand to day, we undertake to trace back
true religion and liberty among men, the clue, with
various windings through broad and beautiful val-
leys, along narrow defiles, steep, rugged, and fright-
ful, over hilltops, radiant with light and glory, and
across dark and gloomy swamps, foul with the stench
of every poison, will lead us, at last, to the door of
the tent of him, of whom God had said of old, "For
I know him, that he will command his children and
his household after him, and they shall keep the way
of the Lord, to do justice and judgment."   Or, if we

go back to Abraham's day, and take up the Abrahamic faith, embracing obedience to God, and justice
to man, and trace it downward `through the ages,
we shall find it branching out among the nations,
and including all the true religion and liberty that
has prevailed on the earth. And so we shall find
the germ, the root-stock, of all earth's true religion
and liberty to have been the faith described in our
text-verse, which dwelt in father Abraham. This
faith had in it the power of an endless life. It was
destined to expand, and finally fill the earth.

In the wise administration of the Divine Government, this Abrahamic germ of true religion and liberty, this Abrahamic faith, embracing in it that
pure worship of the living God, which seeks truly
to keep the righteous way of the Lord, and that true
brotherhood love, which seeks to do justice to individual men in the deep sense of absolute truth, was
destined to descend for many generations, almost
exclusively in the line of the natural descendants of
Abraham, the Jews. But the living power of this
root-stock of godliness and justice kept idolatry and
slavery out of the great Patriarch's own household;
it kept these great iniquities, except as occasional
crimes, out of the Hebrew family and nation, in all
after generations. Neither of these abominations
could possibly exist in conjunction with the Abrahamic godliness and justice. They never did.

But it is a remarkable fact in the history of other
nations, families, and races, that, as they multiplied
and advanced, they degenerated into gross and hope-

less idolatry, and within them the worst forms of oppression prevailed, as established practices. In them, the poor, and the weak, the common people, were degraded, oppressed, and enslaved by the rich and powerful, and for them there was no help. Society became broken up into castes and aristocracies, powers and laws fell into the hands of the higher and stronger, who were not slow to compel the lower and weaker to toil for them, and serve them. But, in Israel, the power of the Abrahamic faith of godliness and justice secured the true worship, and personal liberty and manhood for every individual soul. It protected the poor and weak, and demanded justice for them, and so made slavery impossible.

In process of time, Messiah came, and the true kingdom of Israel, with its Abrahamic faith of godliness and justice, was taken from the Jews, and given to the Gentiles. According to the Scriptures, the Abrahamic faith was identical with the Gospel faith. The Abrahamic faith, then, illuminated and enlarged by the coming and teachings of Christ, transferred to the Gentiles, made a new spiritual Israel among the Gentiles, identical in faith and substance with spiritual Israel of old, among the Jews. So, then, Abraham "is the father of us all," who "keep the way of the Lord," and "do justice and judgment" to men, under both dispensations, both Jews and Gentiles. And as the living power of the Abrahamic faith, the root-stock of godliness and justice among men, kept slavery and idolatry, except as occasional crimes, out of the Hebrew family and nation, so the expansion of this faith in the gospel of Jesus, Abraham's son, is destined to destroy slavery and idolatry everywhere, and ultimately to bring the entire race, wandering Jews and benighted Gentiles, round back to the true Abrahamic worship, love, and justice. When Jehovah said, "I know him, that he will command his children and his household after him, and they shall keep the way of the Lord, to do justice and judgment, that the Lord may bring upon Abraham that which he hath spoken of him," Abraham was constituted the spiritual father of all the true Jehovah worshipers, man lovers, and free peoples under heaven. At the same time, the decree went forth out of the mouth of the Lord, that true religion and true liberty should live and flourish on the earth. The foundations of an everlasting kingdom were then laid, having this seal that the word of the Lord standeth sure. Kingdoms and thrones may be subverted and disappear, old earths and old heavens may pass away with a great noise, the sun may be darkened, and the moon turned into blood, but the true Abrahamic, Apostolic, Puritanic, Evangelical faith, obedience to God, and justice to man, can never be shaken. This great and sublime pledge God gave to Abraham, and to the universe, when he uttered the declaration and prophecy which we are now contemplating.

Obedience to God and justice to man, that is the Abrahamic creed, that is the Gospel creed, that is the creed of the universal kingdom of God. It was this creed, adopted and practiced in Abraham's family, that kept idolatry and slavery out of it, and true worship and freedom in it, and so made it a model, not only for the Jewish nation, but for the world; this same creed, everywhere underlying the Mosaic code, kept idolatry and slavery out of the Jewish nation; and this same creed, by virtue of its own spiritual life-power, keeps slavery out of the circle of a pure gospel faith and practice everywhere. And when this sublime Abrahamic, evangelical, radically anti-slavery creed, has accomplished its whole great mission on the earth, the mission which it began in Abraham and his household, the gospel prayer, "Thy kingdom come," will be answered. Idolatry and slavery will no more curse the earth. The blessing of Abraham will then be upon all the families of the earth.

Such, as we understand it, is the import, and such the breadth of this testimony in regard to Abraham. Religion and liberty had a grand exemplification in the old Patriarch's household, such as made it fit that he should be made the divinely constituted father and founder, not merely of the Jewish nation, but of that more peculiar, holier, and more royal nation, whose badge of citizenship is supreme love to God, and equal and impartial love to man.

And we here record our solemn protest as against a great wrong, against that stupendous perversion of the Divine Word, which makes Abraham, the divinely constituted father and founder of earth's true religion and liberty, the father and founder of earth's most tremendous villainy, chattel slavery. We devoutly hope there is repentance and forgiveness somewhere for those who have handled the Word of God so badly as to have "added" this ruinous perversion "to the things that are written" in the Holy Book.

CHAPTER X.

ANCIENT DARKNESS AND MODERN LIGHT—MODERN DARKNESS AND ANCIENT LIGHT.

A CERTAIN writer has remarked that it has been aptly said that "if Abraham were now living among us he would be put in the penitentiary for bigamy." Possibly. But if the shade of the old Patriarch should now stand forth in our presence, and give his testimony concerning modern affairs, we venture the opinion that he would not hesitate to testify that "if certain slaveholding doctors of theology in young America had lived in his day, they would have been stoned to death for stealing men and women and making merchandise of them."

And when we pertly ask, "Shall we go back to study morality in the twilight of the Patriarchal age?" we fancy we can hear the rebound of the stern echo from their venerable souls, "Shall we, to whom Jehovah spoke face to face, go forward to the

twilight darkness of American slaveholding ethics,
to be instructed in morality? and to learn true justice and judgment?

CHAPTER XI.

CONDITION OF THE JEWS IN EGYPT.

WE devote a section to this topic chiefly for the
purpose of correcting a very general mistake. This
mistake has been corrected repeatedly by others;
but it still prevails, and the correction needs to be
repeated. It is very common for people to suppose
that the condition of the Jews in Egypt, in the time
of Moses, was that of chattel slavery. This supposition arises, probably, from the fact that the terms
employed to describe the oppressions of the Hebrews
in Egypt, are such as have been commonly understood to refer to a state of chattel slavery. The
mischief of this supposition lies in the fact that
people conclude that if the Hebrews were slaves in
Egypt, then, when the language which is applied to
them in describing their condition is applied to
others, they also must have been slaves. The reasoning is, that if the Hebrews in Egypt, in the days
of Moses, were slaves, and so were called "bondmen,"
then all others who are called "bondmen" were
slaves.

But all this is an entire mistake, as has been most abundantly and conclusively shown by Mr· Weld, Mr. Barnes, and others, The Hebrews were not chattel slaves in Egypt, but oppressed freemen: and hence all the language that is applied to them is such as can be properly applied to freemen. The use of such language is nowhere evidence that those to whom it was applied were chattel slaves.

We quote, mostly from the writers alluded to above, the following brief summary of considerations which prove, beyond all contradiction, that the Hebrews were not held as chattel slaves by the Egyptians.

(1.) The Israelites were not dispersed among the families of Egypt, but formed a separate community. Gen. lvi: 34; Ex. viii: 22, 24; ix: 26; x: 23; xi: 7; iv: 29; ii: 9; xvi: 22; xvii: 5; vi: 14. (2.) They had the exclusive possession of the land of Goshen, the best part of the land of Egypt. Gen. lv: 18; lvii: 6, 11, 27; Ex. viii: 22; ix: 26; xii: 4. Goshen must have been at a considerable distance from those parts of Egypt inhabited by the Egyptians. (3.) They lived in permanent dwellings. These were *houses* and not *tents*. In Ex. xii: 7, 22, the two side *posts*, and the upper door *posts*, and the lintel of the houses are mentioned. Each family seems to have occupied a house *by itself.* Acts vii: 20. (4.) They owned "flocks and herds" and "very much cattle." Ex. xii: 4, 6, 32, 37, 38. From the fact that *"every man"* was commanded to kill either a lamb or a kid, one year old, for the Passover, be-

9

fore the people left Egypt, we infer that even the poorest of Israelites owned a flock either of sheep or goats. (5.) They had their own form of government, and preserved their tribe and family divisions, and their internal organization throughout, though still a province of Egypt and *tributary* to it. Ex. ii: 1; xii: 19, 21; vi: 14, 25; v: 19; iii: 16, 18. (6.) They had, in considerable measure, the disposal of their own time. Ex. iii: 16, 18; xii: 6; ii: 9; iv: 27, 29–31. (7.) They were all armed. Ex. xxxii: 27. (8.) All the females seem to have known something of domestic refinements. They were familiar with instruments of music, and skilled in the working of fine fabrics, Ex. xv: 20; xxxv: 25, 26; and both males and females were able to read and write. Deut. xi: 18–20; xvii: 19; xxvii: 3. (9.) Service seems to have been exacted from none but adult males. Nothing is said from which the bond service of females could be inferred; the hiding of Moses three months by his mother, and the payment of wages to her by Pharaoh's daughter, go against such a supposition. Ex. ii: 29. (10.) Their food was abundant, and of great variety. Ex. xii: 15, 39.

"Probably but a small portion of the people were in the service of the Egyptians at any one time. Ex. ix: 26. Besides, when Eastern nations employed tributaries, it was as now, in the use of the levy, requiring them to furnish a given quota, drafted off periodically, so that comparatively but a small portion of the nation would be absent *at any one time.* The adult males of the Israelites were probably divided into companies, which relieved each other at stated intervals of weeks or months."

The above presents, beyond all question, a correct view of the condition of the Israelites in Egypt in the time of Moses. They were tributaries to the Egyptian government; and a tax, in labor or otherwise, was laid upon them for the benefit of that government, which was increased till it became insupportable. It was in this way, and not as chattel slaves, that they were oppressed in Egypt. They were a nation of unchattelized freemen oppressed with a grievous burden of governmental exactions, unrighteous, indeed, and designed to crush them. Now this oppression, which never reached the extent of chattel slavery, is everywhere condemned in the Bible in the strongest language. The Israelites are frequently referred to it, as an example of warning to them, that they should not vex or oppress the stranger. Terrible judgments were visited upon the Egyptians for practicing it. How, then, can we believe, that a few months later, the same Almighty Jehovah, who whelmed the Egyptians in the Red Sea for their wickedness in thus oppressing the Israelites, expressly permitted, and positively ordered them, to reduce to a worse bondage, whomsoever of the heathen they might please? But this we must believe and swallow, if the sort of servitude which is regulated in the Mosaic code was chattel slavery. Μὴγένοιτο! God forbid!

And our belief can not be much better if it was any sort of oppressive servitude. Nay, verily. The overthrow of Pharaoh and his hosts in the waters of the Red Sea is a divine guarantee that no provision will be found in the Mosaic code for any sort of oppression or trespass upon manhood rights. The wrath that gleamed forth from the awful cloud back upon the Egyptian hosts as they approached the fatal shore, is the same wrath which the Word of God everywhere thunders across the track of all oppression.

CHAPTER XII.

THE MOSAIC CODE.

Introduction.

MOSES, and the Jews of his day, were the direct and acknowledged descendants of the old Jewish Patriarchs. Their customs, habits, and modes of thought were, of course, strongly Abrahamic and Patriarchal. The family model which they had received from their fathers, with their great father, Abraham, at the head, was the compound Patriarchal household. The legislation of Moses was designed, of course, to meet and match this family arrangement, and the state of society growing out of it. This legislation will meet and match no other form of society.

Let it be especially noticed here, that no other

classes of servants are recognized in the Mosaic code than those which are alluded to in the Patriarchal history. The legislation of Moses was for the Hebrew tribe, with its Abrahamic family constitution. It sought to regulate the free Jewish household, without disturbing the Patriarchal tendency which still existed among the people. That tendency, which was rather cherished than otherwise, by Moses, though considerably limited and circumscribed, was, as we have seen, to a large household, with all the members closely allied and devoted to the head or Patriarch thereof. These several classes of *attaches*, called servants, which made up the Patriarchal household, were all recognized, as we shall see, in the Mosaic legislation, and their rights carefully provided for and guarded.

CHAPTER XIII.

PARTICULAR EXAMINATION OF VARIOUS PASSAGES IN
THE MOSAIC CODE WHICH REFER TO SERVITUDE.

SEC. 1.—*Circumstances in which the Mosaic Code
was given.*

THE Mosaic code was given immediately after the
departure of the Jews from the land of Egypt.   We
use the term, *immediately*, here with some latitude,
meaning by it that the giving of the law was the
next important thing in the history of the Jews
after their departure from Egypt.   It is not essential
to this discussion whether this period be considered
forty years or less.   It is manifest that immediately
after the deliverance from Egypt, and the passage of
the Red Sea, the giving of the law commenced.   *As
the Jews were* when they left the eastern shore of the
Red Sea, so were they when they received the Mosaic code.   There was no intervening chapter of
history to change or modify their condition, socially,
individually, or collectively.

Now it is manifest that they came out of Egypt
a free people; free as a nation, and free as individuals.   Indeed, there is not the least shadow of evidence that there was any approach to chattel slavery
among them.   It is very plain from the history, that

the Israelites, Jacob and his family, went from Canaan down into Egypt a band of unchattelized freemen. It is as plain that they neither had, nor could have had, slaves, while they were in Egypt. It is preposterous to suppose that they either made slaves of the Egyptians, or captured people from surrounding nations, and made slaves of them in Egypt. It is, therefore, certain, that they carried no slaves with them up out of Egypt. They had not been slaves to the Egyptians, and they were not slaves to each other. Indeed, one of the leading purposes which God had in view in their oppression in Egypt was, to teach them "the heart of the stranger;" and to beget in them a heart to feel for the poor and oppressed, and to deliver them effectually and fully from the spirit of all oppression. And it is especially worthy of notice, that, in their subsequent history, God often appeals to their afflictions in Egypt as a reason why they should "love the stranger" as themselves, and take care not to "vex or oppress" him. It is preposterous in the extreme, to suppose that, in the midst of these circumstances, they came forth from their Egyptian house of bondage a nation of slaveholders. And it seems to us passing strange that Mr. Barnes, as well as other writers, after proving that the words "*servant*," "*buy*," and "*sell*," and other similar words which are used in the Patriarchal history and Mosaic code, determine nothing as to the existence of slavery, these terms being just as applicable to free servants as to slave servants, should adopt, as the basis of all

his reasonings on the subject of Old Testament servitude, the baseless and absurd assumption that the
Israelites were led of God up out of Egypt with a
gang of slaves at their heels. The truth is, they
came out of Egypt a *nation of freemen, with Hebrew
customs and usages, and as Hebrew families;* for
their families were not broken up in Egypt. They
came out both as free, and as free Hebrews. They
did not depart from Egypt as Greeks, or Romans,
or Persians, or Anglo-Saxons, or Frenchmen, but as
ancient Hebrews, with Jewish feelings, customs, and
peculiarities. *They brought the Hebrew family with
them.* As such, without slavery, Moses found them
on the eastern shore of the Red Sea; as such, they
submitted themselves to his leadership, and, as such
he, under divine direction, made laws for them.
What Moses found of servitude among the Israelites
to regulate and to legislate about, was not chattel
slavery, but the free, righteous servitude of the
Abrahamic household, descended in the Jewish families. With this fact, as we shall see, the entire
Mosaic code perfectly agrees.

SEC. 2.—*Institution of the Passover.*—Ex. xii: 43–47.

"And the Lord said unto Moses and Aaron, This
is the ordinance of the passover: there shall no
stranger eat thereof: But every man's servant that
is bought for money, when thou hast circumcised
him, then shall he eat thereof. A foreigner and a
hired servant shall not eat thereof. In one house

shall it be eaten; thou shalt not carry forth aught of the flesh abroad out of the house; neither shall ye break a bone thereof. All the congregation of Israel shall keep it."

These verses are found in the chapter which gives an account of the institution of the Passover. The object of that account is to explain the ordinance of the Passover, and give directions for its observance. The passage which we have quoted is not a statute respecting servitude, and is here examined only because it contains incidental allusion to the different elements of the Hebrew household. It is worthy of notice, that, as in the account of the institution of the rite of circumcision, the different elements of the Hebrew family are alluded to, not to describe them, but for the purpose of defining and limiting the observance of the Passover; and that just as if these constitutive elements of the family were well underderstood. We have here, as in the other case, the family proper, consisting of the children proper, and the other children "born in the house," the "bought-with-money" servant, and, in addition, the "hired servant." The hired servant did not belong to the household, being only a temporary laborer, having his home somewhere else; hence he is not mentioned at all in connection with the rite of circumcision, and hence he is excluded from the Passover.

It is further worthy of remark, that the feast of the Passover was to be eaten *by families*. The lamb was not to be divided to be eaten in different houses.

As the Chaldee has it, "In one society shall ye eat
it." For the sake of social fellowship, and to make
the idea of the family prominent, each family, as a
family, were to eat the Passover together. Hence
it took in all the bona-fide members of the household. The "bought-with-money" servant was a fix-
ture of the household, for the time being, and so
belonged to it, as part and parcel of it. The phrase,
"bought with money," as applied to him in Mosaic
diction, has not the remotest allusion to his being a
slave. That ancient phraseology only shows how he
became attached to the household. As we have
already seen, this was a common mode, in Patriarchal
times, of attaching servants to the household. This
phrase, in its origin and use in the Hebrew language, related to freemen, and a state of freedom,
and not at all to slaves, and a state of slavery. No
ancient Israelite would think for a moment of referring it to slaves. It has come to be referred to
slaves only by lugging back the sense of modern
usage, and botching it on to the honest ancient Hebrew. And so the Word of God is perverted and
carried over to the abominable service of giving its
holy sanction to chattel slavery. But let the reader
note and remember, that we find no other elements
belonging to the Hebrew household mentioned anywhere in the Mosaic writings, than these which belonged to the Abrahamic household. In that household, as we have seen, these elements must have
been free elements. They are nowhere described as
being any thing else. They belonged to the Abra-

hamic household; they belonged to the Hebrew family afterward; and to them the Mosaic legislation everywhere corresponds.

Sec. 3.—*Hebrew Servants.*

Ex. xxi: 2–6—"If thou buy a Hebrew servant, six years shall he serve: and in the seventh he shall go out free for nothing: If he came in by himself, he shall go out by himself: if he were married, then his wife shall go out with him. If his master have given him a wife, and she have borne him sons or daughters; the wife and her children shall be her master's, and he shall go out by himself. And if the servant shall plainly say, I love my master, my wife, and my children; I will not go out free: Then his master shall bring him unto the judges; he shall also bring him to the door or unto the door-post; and his master shall bore his ear through with an awl; and he shall serve him forever."

In regard to this statute, observe as follows:

1. In form, language, and spirit, it is a direct and positive statute.

2. There is a partial exposition of this statute by the great Jewish Lawgiver himself, where it is repeated in Deuteronomy, which throws great light upon it. This rehearsal is as follows: Deut. xv: 12–18—"And if thy brother, a Hebrew man, or a Hebrew woman, be sold unto thee, and serve thee six years; then in the seventh year thou shalt let

him go free from thee.   And when thou sendest him
out free from thee, thou shalt not let him go away
empty: Thou shalt furnish him liberally out of thy
flock, and out of thy floor, and out of thy wine-press:
of that wherewith the Lord thy God hath blessed
thee thou shalt give unto him.   And thou shalt remember that thou wast a bondman in the land of
Egypt, and the Lord thy God redeemed thee: therefore I command thee this thing to-day.   And it
shall be, if he say unto thee, I will not go away
from thee; because he loveth thee and thine house,
because he is well with thee; Then thou shalt take
an awl and thrust it through his ear unto the door,
and he shall be thy servant forever.   And also unto
thy maid-servant thou shalt do likewise.   It shall
not seem hard unto thee, when thou sendest him
away free from thee; for he hath been worth a
double hired servant to thee, in serving thee six
years: and the Lord thy God shall bless thee in all
that thou doest."

3. It is manifest from these two passages, taken
together, as referring to one and the same statute,
as they evidently do, that this statute, in regard to
Hebrew servants, included alike in its provisions
both *male and female* servants.   The recapitulation
in Deuteronomy, where express mention is made of
female servants, as well as of male servants, makes
this positively certain.

4. It is further evident, from the nature of the
case, that Hebrew servants, such as this statute contemplates, would generally, if not universally, belong

to a class of people who were otherwise *destitute of any home.* Those who had homes of their own would not need, and would not be likely, to engage as servants, except as "hired servants."

This is also clearly evident from the regulations in regard to the Passover. The Passover was peculiarly a *family* institution. The mere temporary, "hired servant," who was supposed to have a home somewhere else, was forbidden to eat of it in the family of his employer. The servant "bought with money," such as was the servant contemplated in this statute in regard to Hebrew servants, which we are now considering, having no other home, was to eat of it in the family in which he was servant. Hebrew servants that were "bought," then, under the provisions of this statute, were generally if not universally, servants that were destitute of a home.

5. It is also plain that, in the contract for service contemplated in this statute, the Hebrew servant was received and incorporated into the family as part and parcel of it. This, indeed, as we have already seen, was an important and leading element in this engagement between master and servant. It was an alliance of the servant with the household, to become a member of it. It was more than simple hire. It was a contract for household membership.

6. The word "buy," in these passages, has its usual sense, when applied to the engagement of servants. It refers simply to the money stipulation between the householder and the homeless person, by which the alliance of the latter with the former,

as a household member, was effected. It has no allusion whatever to property ownership in the person of the servant. It refers to the bargain made between the householder and the servant, in which the former paid money to the latter, and by which the latter became a member of the household, to do service, and be under its control. In the repetition and expansion of this statute, in Deut., chapter xv, this is clearly implied. In the twelfth verse the phraseology is, "And if thy brother, a Hebrew man, or a Hebrew woman *be sold* unto thee." The verb used here, and translated *"be sold,"* is translated, in Lev. xxy: 47, "sell himself." A similar translation of this same verb may be found in Isa. l: 1, and lii: 3, and in Jer. xxxiv: 14. That the servant himself received the money paid, is also conclusively manifest from Lev. xxv: 51, 52; from which it is also manifest that it was the custom for the servant to receive his pay for the whole six years' service in advance, at the time the contract was made. The servant, therefore, as a free man, made his part of the bargain, and, as a free man, entered upon the fulfillment of the contract: his pay he received in advance. The householder, also, as a free man, and as with a free man, made his part of the bargain, and fulfilled it accordingly. There was no compulsion on either side, nor any other element of slavery.

7. All this agrees perfectly with the peculiar constitution of the Jewish household, and the customs of Jewish society. The contract between the

Hebrew servant and his employer was not exactly like a modern bargain between a laborer and his employer. It was, by no means, so exclusively a mere, dry, money transaction. It had in it more of the friendly, neighborly, social, family element. It was a contract for service: it was also a contract for *home* and its attendant privileges and blessings.

8. Hence the engagement *was extended through several years*. Attachment to the household in the Abrahamic, Jewish sense, must have some measure of permanency connected with it, in order to be of any value as a household connection. It must extend through several years, in order to be really valuable to either servant or master. Otherwise, it would be a mere temporary matter, as in the case of "hired servants." The arrangement contemplated in this statute was a very different thing from that which pertained to "hired servants." "Hired servants" did not properly belong to the household, but were merely engaged to do temporary service, with a home somewhere else: or, at least, without a home in the household where they were employed. The servants provided for in this statute constituted another class entirely. They were, by the opening contract, incorporated into the household as part and parcel of it. This would demand some measure of permanency in the arrangement. Hence the extension of the time to six years: the shortest allowable period consistent with the nature of the case.

9. But, for several reasons, such an arrangement needed *some limitation*. First, in order to give all

servants an opportunity to establish *a home of their own*. It was a favorite object with the Mosaic code, and the whole Jewish Dispensation, to elevate every man and procure for him a home People that were destitute of such home could find a temporary, partial home, under this statute for servitude. To give them an opportunity of establishing an independent one of their own, this servitude arrangement for a home was limited to six years: at the end of which it was caused to expire, in order to give the servant a chance to try for himself, or renew the servitude arrangement, as might please him best. The best arrangement for every man is to have a home of his own: next to that, is a home in some other good home. This latter was the thing contemplated and sought after in this statute, for such persons as were not able to secure for themselves the former. The time was extended to six years, in order to make the connection as home-like as possible: it was limited to six years, in order to give every servant an opportunity to make a home for himself.

Secondly, this arrangement was limited, lest it should run into slavery, or some other form of oppression. This limitation most effectually forestalled all slavery as to Hebrew servants among the Jews. Again, it is also very probable that this statute had another limitation. It is altogether probable that the servant might redeem himself at any time, by a mutual agreement with the master, and on refunding the purchase-money. By express statute, (Lev. xxv: 47–49,) the Hebrew servant sold to "a sojourner or stranger" might be thus redeemed, and the presumption is, that all Hebrew servants, under this statute in Ex. xxi: 2–6, had the same privilege.

10. But if the servant found that his connection with the household was likely to be better for him and his family than any home which he could establish for himself, this statute provided (Ex. xxi: 5–6; Deut. xv: 16–17,) for *permanent* alliance, according to the old Abrahamic custom. "If he say unto thee, I will not go away from thee; because he loveth thee and thine house, because he is well with thee; Then thou shalt take an awl, and thrust it through his ear unto the door, and he shall be thy servant forever."

In Patriarchal times, it is manifest that the alliance with the household to render service and be subject to it, to be a member of it and have a home in it, was usually a *permanent* alliance; for life, and even for future generations. This tendency still remained in the Jewish nation. Hence the need of the special provisions made in this statute, for permanent connection with the household. In all cases this connection was entirely voluntary, and on the basis of freedom. It made no slavery, and contemplated none. It was a permanent membership connection with the household, to be under its control and do service for it, much like that of all the members of the household. This was the Jewish idea of servitude. This was Paul's idea of it, as he expressly tells us. "Now I say, that the heir, as long as he is a child, differeth nothing from a servant."—(Gal.

iv: 1.) But this permanent alliance was strongly guarded in several ways. (1.) It was entered upon only after a long and thorough trial. (2.) The engagement must be made in a public manner, and a public record made of it. (3.) The servant lost no rights of citizenship by this transaction, and hence had equal protection from the laws of the land with the master.

11. If the contract was with married servants, that is, with a man-servant and his wife, at the end of six years they were to go out free together. And in order that they might be assisted, much as parents assist their children in starting in life, in establishing a home for themselves, they were to be "furnished" "liberally" by the master, "out of his flock," and "out of his floor," and "out of his wine-press."—Deut. xv: 14. This was to be done *cheerfully*.—Verse 18. That is, they were to be sent out from the household, where they had so long found a home, with paternal sympathy and help, to build a home for themselves. How beautifully Patriarchal, generous, man-loving, and Christian! infinitely further removed from slavery than the poles are from each other.

12. And the proviso in the fourth verse of the statute, as laid down in Ex. xxi, is in perfect harmony with all the rest. "If his master have given him a wife, and she have borne him sons or daughters; the wife and her children shall be her master's, and he shall go out by himself." It was the universal custom in the days of the Patriarchs, and for

many generations following, that not even a wife could be transferred from one household to another without compensation. The usages of the times compelled every man to "purchase" and pay for his wife. In the case before us, the master is supposed to "give" or furnish the servant a wife: one that already belonged to his household; and hence furnished without compensation. The woman already belonged to the master's household, and the giving of her to the servant to be his wife did not transfer her to any other household. She belonged to the master's household still, as did the servant who was her husband.

Now, it is manifest, from all the circumstances of the case, that she would be thus "given" by the master only on supposition that the servant would remain a permanent member of the household. But if, contrary to this expectation, he should determine to go out by himself, at the end of his six years' term of service, the fixed usages of society, and hence justice to the master, would not permit him to take his wife with him (and of course the children would remain with the mother,) *without the usual arrangements for transfer*. But his going out free by himself, that is, alone, would, by no means, separate him from his wife in the sense of divorce. Such departure from the household would not in the least disturb the relation of husband and wife. It would separate them only as to home and household. And even this inconvenience could be easily remedied.

It could always be remedied, (1,) by the servant's

consenting to remain permanently a member of the household, a privilege which he always had a right to claim, and the claiming of which would manifestly be implied in his marriage contract: (2,) by his paying the usual dowry and for whatever of unexpired service might remain due to the master from the wife: (3,) by his waiting till his wife herself should be free, provided she was a six years' servant, and not a permanent servant. It could always be forestalled and avoided by the servant's refusing to form any such matrimonial engagement. The presumption therefore is, that the separation alluded to would usually be the result of perverseness on the part of the servant. His connection with his wife would be formed in view of the circumstances of the case, and if he was an honest and honorable man, need not involve the necessity of any separation at all. His master would give him a wife in order to bind him to the household: his acceptance would be his consent to his master's object.

This statute, therefore, either in its spirit or in the letter thereof, either in its general scope or in its particular provisions, does not lie in the same hemisphere with chattel slavery. There is not in it any sort of slavery. Its provisions are wise, benevolent, and on the basis of the fullest individual freedom. Hence its direct, positive, and permanent character. It is not a statute to permit an evil till some other and different legislation should work to remove it, but a positive law authorizing and establishing forever, on principles of righteousness and truth, that which it concerns. Its object was to secure personal freedom, protect individual manhood rights, and promote the welfare and happiness of all. All its provisions were wise for the accomplishment of this end.

SEC. 4.—*Special Case of Contract for Service and Anticipated Marriage.*

Ex. xxi: 7–11—"And if a man sell his daughter to be a maid-servant, she shall not go out as the men-servants do. If she please not her master, who hath betrothed her to himself, then shall he let her be redeemed: to sell her unto a strange nation he shall have no power, seeing he hath dealt deceitfully with her. And if he have betrothed her unto his son, he shall deal with her after the manner of daughters. If he take him another *wife*, her food, her raiment, and her duty of marriage, shall he not diminish. And if he do not these three unto her, then shall she go out free without money."

1. The key to the exposition of this somewhat difficult passage of Scripture is to be found in its *speciality*. From the peculiar constitution of the Jewish household, and of Jewish society, cases might arise in which it might be desirable for the father and his family to seek a place for his daughter in some other household, to do service for it and be a member of it, with the expressed or implied understanding that she should, at some future time, be-

come a wife in it. This would constitute a very
peculiar and special case, requiring a special statute,
and special safeguards. This is the case provided
for in the statute before us: a case of contract for
service and anticipated marriage.

2. It is manifest, from the nature of the case, that
instances of this sort would not be very numerous.
In ordinary circumstances, fathers would not "sell"
their daughters for service and anticipated marriage.
The usual practice was to "sell" daughters in actual
marriage. Daughters would, much more commonly,
remain in the paternal homestead till transferred to
another household by actual marriage. Nevertheless, the father might, sometimes, find it desirable
to transfer his daughter to another household, to be
a member of it, and do service in it, if he had good
reason to believe that the change would result in a
matrimonial alliance with the lord of the house, or
with his son. To provide for, and guard such cases,
was the object of this statute.

3. Since, therefore, this was a case of contract for
service and anticipated marriage, it comes under the
rules both for service and marriage. This fact
brings in the father's agency. This agency is to be
understood, of course, only in the voluntary sense,
according to the prevailing usages of the times and
of Jewish society. It implied no compulsion anywhere. Modern usage makes the father *give* away
his daughter in marriage, and a dowry along with
her. Ancient usage made the father "sell" his
daughter and take the dowry. The former gives

the money, or pay; the latter took it. Neither the modern "giving," nor the ancient "selling," implies any compulsion on the part of the father. The selling of the daughter, in the case before us, as alluded to in the seventh verse, was precisely as usual when a father sold his daughter in marriage, and had not the remotest allusion whatever to property possession in the person of the daughter, on the part of either the father or the master. It was a selling for marriage at some future time, and for service and membership in the household meanwhile. Neither of these contracts among the Jews ever had the remotest connection with chattel slavery. Freedom was always the basis of both. When Boaz "purchased" Ruth, the great-grandmother of David, and ancestral mother of Messiah, it was not as a slave, or to be a slave, but as a free woman, to be a wife. Such purchase was a part of the customary courtship, and was conducted on principles of the most generous and honorable gallantry. It was entirely voluntary on all sides, and implied no compulsion anywhere. The fact that the father "sells" his daughter, in the two-fold contract for service and marriage, has not the remotest allusion to a state of slavery.

4. This statute treats of the "*going out*" of this particular class of servants referred to. "And if a man sell his daughter to be a maid-servant, *she shall not go out as the men-servants do.*" This is the subject of the statute. It treats of the *going out* of this particular class of maid-servants.

The contrast here is not between *maid*-servants and *men*-servants, as the reader might at first suppose; but manifestly between this particular class of maid-servants, and the six years' man-servants and maid-servants alluded to in the preceding statute. The phrase, "she shall not go out as the men-servants do," plainly refers back to the servants spoken of in the preceding statute. But this statute, as we have before seen, includes both men-servants and maid-servants. Inasmuch, therefore, as the Hebrew word for "men-servants" in the phrase, "she shall not go out as the men-servants do," is a general term, and may include both men-servants and maid-servants, it is clear that the contrast here is between this particular class of maid-servants, and the men-servants and maid-servants described and legislated for in the preceding statute. These were six years' Hebrew servants, both male and female. They were to "go out" at the expiration of the six years' term of service; that was the way in which they should "go out." At that time, they were to go out free, liberally furnished. Now, the daughter, transferred according to this special statute we are now considering, should not go out in this way. She should not be subject to the rules laid down for common servants. The contract, in her case, embraced also the marriage contract. The daughter thus allied to the household should not be sent away as the common six years' servants were. Her term of service was expected to lose itself in the conjugal relation, either with the master, or with his son. In case of any failure in this—in case the master should not fix upon her for his wife, (Hebrew,) nor yet his son, according to the original expectation, and in case she was not treated as an espoused wife, she should not be sent away as the common servants were. Different rules should apply to her case.

Before examining these several regulations separately in order, it is worthy of remark that they all look to the protection of the maid-servant. The design of this whole statute plainly was to guard and protect her rights. This it does effectually. It fully protects her rights as a free woman.

1. It is manifestly implied in this statute, that it was the expectation, in the premises, that the master would ultimately marry the maid-servant, and she would become his wife. "If she please not her master who hath betrothen her unto himself." If the master should act in good faith, and actually make her his wife, well. The servant would be lost in the wife, and there would be no "going out" at all.

2. But "if she please not her master," as soon as it appears that the master does not fix upon her for a wife, and thus there is a failure to consummate the principal object of the original contract, namely, marriage, then, the master "shall let," or cause "her to be redeemed." If the master should fail in this part of his obligation, then the maid-servant should "go out" by redemption. This is the first regulation in this statute in regard to her going forth from the household of the master who had

11

"bought" her. If he failed in the marriage contract, this failure should forfeit all right to retain
her as a mere maid-servant; nor should he have any
power to transfer her, either for service or for marriage, to any other *family*, for this is clearly the
sense of the word translated *"nation,"* in this eighth
verse. The master should have no power to dispose
of her to any one else for a wife, for the purpose
of recovering a portion, or all, of the dowry which
he had paid for her. This right of disposal should
continue to lie exclusively with her own proper
family.

3. In the third place, if the woman should be betrothed to the son of the master, in anticipation of
marriage, all would be well. In this case, also, the
contract for service would lose itself in the marriage
relation, according to the original expectation, and
there would be no "going out" in the case. As
the wife of the son, the master of the household
should treat her as a daughter. "He" should "deal
with her after the manner of daughters."

4. But if there should be a failure as to the marriage contract on the part of both master and son,
and "another" female (the Hebrew does not say
"wife,") should be taken into the household, as she
had been at first, with a view to anticipated marriage, thus supplanting her entirely in this respect,
then, if she is either not able to accomplish her redemption, or does not desire to do so, she shall be
treated in all respects as an honorable member of
the household. Her home there, her food, and her

clothing, shall be faithfully furnished. The Hebrew word, translated "her duty of marriage," in the tenth verse, is probably used in no other place in the Bible.* The root from which it is derived means "*to dwell;*" and hence the signification, "dwelling-place," or "home," which we give to it in this passage.

We object to the sense of the English translation, as being unsuitable to the passage. All the provisions of this statute respect time *previous* to marriage, and refer to failure in the marriage part of the contract. This statute, mark, includes simply the case of the daughter sold *to be a maid-servant*, with marriage anticipated, and treats of her "going out," or release from the household, not as a repudiated wife, but *as a maid-servant*. It is not at all a case of divorce, but of release from service, when certain conditions have transpired. The scope of the statute clearly locates these conditions previous to actual marriage. For marriage absorbs the service contract, and puts an end to all going out *as a maid-servant*. All departure from the household, after marriage, must be as a repudiated wife, which is a matter altogether foreign to the title and subject of this statute. First, if marriage takes place between the master and the maid-servant, of course, there is to be no departure. Second, if the master fails as to the marriage, then the maid-servant may go out from the household and its service, by re-

* Some suppose that this same word occurs in Hos. x: 10, where it is translated "*furrows;*" margin, "*habitations.*"

demption. Third, if the master betroth her unto his son, she is to be in the household as a daughter. Fourth, if the master "take him another," not in actual marriage, but as the first was taken, to displace her so far as anticipated marriage is concerned, the maid-servant, instead of securing her redemption, might complete her service contract, if she chose, provided she should be furnished with food, and raiment, and home, that is, home privileges, as an honorable member of the household.

5. But if these should be diminished, (verse 11th,) this should forfeit all claim on the part of the master, and she should be at liberty to "go out" "free without money," her service contract being cancelled without the payment of any redemption money whatever. As a maid-servant released from obligation, by the failure of the master to perform his part of the contract, should she "go out." The original contract really included in it food, raiment, and home, as betrothed wife or daughter: failure in any of these particulars should release the maid-servant from all further obligations. Such failure would be a virtual violation of the whole spirit of the original contract, which neither contemplated nor admitted of any degradation of the maiden. That contract secured for her an honorable transfer from the paternal home to another household, eventually to become the wife of the lord thereof, or of his son.

Now, that this is a case of freedom, and not of slavery, is sufficiently manifest on the very face of things.

1. It is perfectly certain, at the outset, that no Hebrew father would ever enter into such an arrangement as this, unless both father and daughter had good reason to believe that the alliance would be for the advantage of the daughter and her family. The "seller," in this case, is a Hebrew *father*, and not a Southern slave-dealer. The arrangement is that of a Hebrew *father* for his beloved daughter, of the stock of Abraham. God forbid that we should for a moment imagine that any father in Israel should, for an instant, harbor the thought of consigning his own daughter to the condition of a chattel slave! Such a base slander upon the seed of Abraham finds no warrant from the Sacred Record, and should not be tolerated for a single moment.

2. There is a total want of all positive evidence in this statute, that a state of slavery was contemplated therein. The "selling" implies no such evidence: the being "a maid-servant" implies no such evidence: the fact of redemption from service implies no such evidence: the going out free without money implies no such evidence. Not one particle of such evidence can be found in this whole statute.

3. The main, if not the whole object of this statute, was to protect and guard the rights of the maid-servant as a free woman. This protection is totally inconsistent with a state of chattel slavery. This is too manifest to need further illustration or proof.

4. It may be noticed further, that no lower social condition, or position, is contemplated in this statute

for the maid-servant than that of wife, or daughter. The purchase was manifestly with a view to marriage with the master himself, or with his son. Failure in this gave her immediate liberty to return to her father's house. How utterly inconsistent all this is with a state of slavery. All the regulations of this statute imply freedom and equality, and are totally inconsistent with the degradation of chattel slavery.

Before dismissing this subject, it should be noticed still further, that the honor of the master and his family would always be pledged in behalf of the safety and welfare of the maid-servant in question, just as is the case in similar transactions in modern times. Being an arrangement between freemen, and having to do with the most sacred relations of life, there would, after all, be less liability to abuse than would, at first sight, appear. We are not, by any means, to understand either that the father would be a cold and hard-hearted Shylock, seeking only to make gain out of the offspring of his own loins, or that the master (more properly family head,) would be only a modern slave-breeder, or a Turkish harem-master. This statute refers to, and contemplates nothing of the kind. It has reference to honest and honorable Hebrew men and women, and was designed to guard the rights of the weaker party. On the side of that weaker party would be both this special statute of protection, and every sentiment of honor and generosity of the other party.

Finally, let it be observed, that a true and consistent exposition of this statute develops neither slavery nor *polygamy*, as contained or provided for in it. Both of these things have been diligently sought after in it, but lo! neither of them is anywhere to be found. The object of the statute is to provide for the release of the maid-servant *from service*, in case of failure in the marriage part of the contract. This is expressly stated in the first verse of the statute. The "going out" is a going out from service, when the marriage alliance *failed*. The provisions all respect time previous to actual marriage, and look simply to the release of the maid-servant from service, on failure in duty of the other party, until we come to the ambiguous phrase "duty of marriage." Now, it is very harsh and unnatural indeed, to suppose that the whole drift of the statute changes, at this point, from a statute for the release of the abused maid-servant from service to a statute for divorce from marriage. As already interpreted, we think the whole statute relates to release from service, and that there is nothing in it that has the remotest allusion to either slavery or polygamy.

SEC. 5.—*Sundry Regulations in Regard to Servants.*

Ex. xxi: 20, 21—"And if a man smite his servant, or his maid, with a rod, and he die under his hand; he shall be surely punished." (Margin, *avenged.*) "Notwithstanding, if he continue a day or two, he shall not be punished: for he is his money."

Two things are enacted in this passage, both of which are entirely consistent with a state of freedom and equal citizenship on the part of the servant: and the first of them implies the fullest equality of the servant with the master, as to manhood rights.

1. If a man should smite his servant to death, he should be punished, or, as the Hebrew has it, be avenged. What this punishment was to be, is to be learned from other statutes. "And he that killeth any man shall surely be put to death."—Lev. xxiv: 17. This settles it, beyond all dispute, that the murder of a servant was to be punished just as was the murder of any other person.

If it be asked why there is this special reference to servants, if they came under the general law in regard to murder, we give a Yankee answer, by referring the reader to the fact that repetitions of particular statutes, and their reference to special cases and particular classes of persons, are very common in the writings of Moses. We need not go far to find examples. In the Decalogue we have the universal statute, "Thou shalt not kill."—Ex. xx: 13. In the very next chapter we have this repeated in another form, referring, perhaps, to the manner of killing, and also stating the penalty: "He that smiteth a man so that he die, shall be surely put to death."—Ex. xxi: 12. A few verses below, we have the particular reference to servants, in the passage we are examining. In Num. xxxv: 16, this same law, in regard to murder, is further particularized in this form : "If he smite him with an instrument of iron, so that he die, he is a murderer : the murderer shall surely be put to death." A little further on, in the same chapter, this is repeated in the universal form with reference to the evidence in the case: " *Whoso killeth any person*, the murderer shall be put to death, by the mouth of witnesses." Now the design of these repetitions and particular references was not to imply that there were exceptions to this law in regard to murder, but to cut off all exceptions, and to reiterate the law with additional solemnity and force. He that smites a servant to death, for example, shall surely be punished : as surely as if he had murdered any other man. The manhood rights of the servant shall not be one whit less sacred than those of the master, or any other man. With God, in his righteous judgments, there is no respect of persons. Surely chattel slavery finds no special countenance in such statutes as this.

2. " Notwithstanding if he continue a day or two, he shall not be punished:" that is, as a murderer, the presumption then being that the master did not intend to kill him. Just as in the statute in the preceding verses: "If men strive together, and one smite another with a stone, or with his fist, and he die not, but keepeth his bed, if he rise again, and walketh abroad upon his staff, then shall he that smote him be quit:" Quit how? and to what extent?

Plainly quit as to the crime of murder, but not quit
as to all blame. The presumption would be that
the smiter did not intend to kill. But this would
by no means release from all blame. Whatever
blame, whatever guilt, whatever mischief might be
involved in the case, would require to be treated
according to statutes and principles applicable to the
case. "Breach for. breach, eye for eye, tooth for
tooth," blemish for blemish. The smiter should,
also, as was just, make up for any pecuniary loss
that might result: "only he shall pay for the loss
of his time, and shall cause him to be thoroughly
healed."

Precisely these same principles should hold in
regard to the servant. If the master should smite
him to death, he should be punished as a murderer.
If the servant should continue a day or two, the
presumption would be that there was no murderous
intent, and the master should be quit of punishment
as a murderer. This presumption would be strength-
ened by the fact that the smiting was "with a rod"
simply, and that the master had a pecuniary interest
in the servant which he would lose if he murdered
him. "For he is his money." We have before seen
that the Hebrew servant was "the money" of the
master, only in the sense of voluntary contract for
services and membership in the household of the
master. The pecuniary loss, if the servant died,
would be the master's, inasmuch as he had paid for
his services in advance, and would be deprived of
those services by the death of the servant.

There is, therefore, nothing in this whole statute which degrades the servant in the least; nothing that conflicts with his equal manhood, and equal citizenship in the Hebrew commonwealth, with the master. This whole statute contemplates him solely as an equal brother man, occupying, for the time being, a subordinate station. No principles of legal treatment are applied to him, which are not applied to other men. Indeed, this whole statute is a statute of protection for the servant. It guards his life from fatal harm, as the Mosaic code guarded the lives of all men, with the terrible penalty of death.

And then, a few verses further along, it was enacted that any serious personal injury done to the servant should forfeit all claim on the part of the master to further services. "And if a man smite the eye of his servant, or the eye of his maid, that it perish, he shall let him go free for his eye's sake. And if he smite out his man-servant's tooth, or his maid-servant's tooth, he shall let him go free for his tooth's sake." This statute reveals the *spirit*—the kind of protection which the Mosaic code extended to the servant. It carefully guarded all his rights, as a man, an equal fellow-citizen; so carefully and sacredly guarded them, that the word servant never came to have a degraded sense in Bible literature; a significant fact, which all pro-slavery interpreters of the Bible would do well to ponder.

Ex. xxi: 32—"If the ox shall push a man-servant, or a maid-servant, he shall give unto their master thirty shekels of silver, and the ox shall be stoned."

Inasmuch as the services of the servant, by mutual compact and just equivalent rendered, belonged to the master, and hence the pecuniary loss would fall upon him, it was but simple justice that the owner of the ox should compensate said master. Here, again, is nothing inconsistent with acknowledged manhood, freedom, and equal citizenship on the part of the servant. This statute respects only the compensation to be given to the master for his pecuniary loss in the services of the servant, for which he had before paid. The other parts of this statute concerning "an ox that pusheth or goreth," were to be applied to servants, in all respects, as to other men.

Ex. xxii: 3—"If he have nothing, then he shall be sold for his theft."

This is the case of the thief who should be found destitute of means by which to make "full restitution" for his theft. It was the law concerning theft, that the thief "should make full restitution" for the wrong committed. If he "had nothing" with which to make restitution, then he should be sold for his theft.

If, now, we assume that he was to be sold as a chattel slave, it will be very easy for us to make this a case of slavery! And it is only on the ground of this baseless assumption that chattel slavery is found in this statute.

If the thief was sold as a free man, to do service until he had worked out "full restitution" for the trespass committed against his neighbor by his theft, as was manifestly the case, this statute reveals not the faintest glimmer of chattel slavery. A small theft would require a shorter term of service, or, if you please, servantship; a larger theft, a longer period.

This, therefore, was a wise and just statute, and trenched upon no inalienable rights or privileges. It has not the remotest reference to chattel slavery.

CHAPTER XIV.

FOREIGN SERVANTS.

Analysis of Lev. xxv *and* xxvi.

THE specific legislation of the Mosaic code in regard to foreign servants, is very brief, being all contained in two verses and a half, found in the twenty-fifth chapter of Leviticus. This short passage of Scripture has suffered many things at the hands of various interpreters. It will be our object, in part, to give the results of modern investigation, hoping thereby to present the true meaning and bearing of the passage in question.

The twenty-fifth and twenty-sixth chapters of Leviticus contain an unbroken message from the Lord to the children of Israel. The twenty-fifth chapter begins with this declaration: "And the Lord spake unto Moses in Mount Sinai, saying." The message following is continuous and unbroken till we reach the last verse of the twenty-sixth chapter, which is this: "These are the statutes, and judgments, and laws, which the Lord made between him and the children of Israel in Mount Sinai by the hand of Moses." The enactment in regard to Hebrew servants occurs near the middle of this continuous message.

In this whole message, contained in these two chapters, several distinct matters are considered. Some of these are closely connected, others are more remotely related, and others, still, have only a very distant connection with each other, if any at all. This fact needs especially to be borne in mind in studying the whole passage, and in studying particular parts of it.

. The following analysis will illustrate the above remark, and help to exhibit the position of the part that refers to foreign servants, and show its connections.

The first subject of enactment and regulation in this message is the sabbatic, or seventh year. This occupies the first seven verses of chapter twenty-fifth.

At the eighth verse the Jubilee is introduced. This was to occur on the fiftieth year, and was to be a great religious festival among the Jews. The fiftieth was to be a sacred year. "Ye shall hallow the fiftieth year."—V. 10. "It shall be holy unto you." —V. 12. It commenced on a day most sacred to the Jews: "On the tenth day of the seventh month, *in the day of atonement.*" The great object of the Jubilee was a *religious one.* Of its whole significance it is not to our present purpose to inquire.

Now, in order to the best observance of this fiftieth year, as a great religious sabbath for all the land, of peculiar sacredness and significance, several special regulations would be needed. 1. Of course it would need to be a year of *rest from labor.* "Ye shall not sow, neither reap that which groweth of itself in it, nor gather the grapes in it of thy vine undressed."— V. 11. 2. "Liberty should be proclaimed throughout all the land unto all the inhabitants thereof."— V. 9. That is, there should be such a finishing up of engagements from one to another, such a settlement and release as would give full freedom to all the people to observe this year, as a sacred sabbath year, to the best advantage. This was not a proclamation for the emancipation of modern slaves; for slaves were unknown to the Jewish commonwealth. (1.) Every man should return to his paternal estate. "And ye shall return every man unto his possession." —V. 10. (2.) Every man should return to his home. "And ye shall return every man unto his family."— V. 10. (3.) All debts were to be limited by the Jubilee.—V. 14–16. Contracts were to be adjusted to the Jubilee, and so regulated as to terminate at that time. Business matters would hence be so settled up at the opening of the Jubilee, that they would not disturb the best observance thereof. (4.) As always, in all this no oppression should be practiced. "Ye shall not oppress one another."—V. 14, 17. The institution of the Jubilee occupies the chapter from the 8th verse to the 17th inclusive.

From verse 18th onward to the 22d, inclusive, further particular directions are given in regard to the seventh, or sabbatic year. In these verses no allusion is made to the Jubilee. The statute ordaining the Jubilee ends with the 17th verse.

Pursuing our analysis of the chapter, we notice

that the next section of the chapter, verses 23–34, contains a statute in regard to *the land*. "The land shall not be sold forever."—V. 23. It might be "sold," (or mortgaged, rather,) however, subject to "redemption." "In all the land of your possession ye shall grant a redemption."—V. 24. But if no one was found able or willing to redeem it, it should revert to the original owner at the Jubilee.—V. 28. This regulation in regard to the land was one of the organic laws of the Jewish commonwealth. The Jubilee was made *the time* when the land that had been "sold" should revert to the original owner. This was one of the beautiful and happy incidental arrangements connected with this great sabbatic year. But it should be observed that this statute contained in these verses (23–34) is a statute *concerning the land*, and not a statute concerning the Jubilee. The Jubilee is alluded to only incidentally, as the *time when* the land should revert to the proper owner, in case of failure to redeem it. The jubilee statute proper is all comprised in verses 8–17.

Let us proceed. Verses 35–38 contain another distinct topic of legislation, in which there is no allusion whatever to the Jubilee. The spirit of this injunction in this section of this message from the Lord to the children of Israel, is so good an example of the spirit of the Mosaic code generally, that we can not forbear quoting it entire: 35. "And if thy brother be waxen poor, and fallen into decay with thee; [margin, his hand faileth;] then thou shalt relieve [strengthen] him: *yea, though he be* a stran-

12

ger or a sojourner; that he may live with thee.
36. Take thou no usury of him, or increase: but fear
thy God; that thy brother may live with thee.
37. Thou shalt not give him thy money upon usury,
nor lend him thy victuals for increase. 38. I am
the Lord your God, which brought you forth out of
the land of Egypt, to give you the land of Canaan,
and to be your God."

"Fallen in decay:" that is, "disabled from helping himself: one who was unable to help himself, as
if his hand were shaking with the palsy." (Bush, *in
loco.*) This, then, is a special statute or injunction
in behalf of that particular class of persons, who,
through bodily infirmities, old age, or other causes,
should become poor, and unable to take care of themselves. Such were to be assisted to maintain their
standing and position as fellow-citizens of the commonwealth of Israel. " That he may live with thee:"
keep his place and maintain himself and family.
This most beneficent injunction is enforced with a
beautiful and affecting allusion, in verse 38th, to
God's authority, and his great goodness to them in
bringing them out of the land of Egypt, and giving
them the land of Canaan, to be their God. A fine
example this of the application of the great law of
love to the case of truly needy people.

Proceeding with our analysis of the chapter, we
come, next in order, (verses 39–43,) to a special statute in regard to another class of poor families, who,
though not disabled, should find it difficult to sustain
themselves, and keep their land and home. A man

with his family in such circumstances, might seek relief by "selling himself." 39. "And if thy brother that dwelleth by thee, be waxen poor, and be sold, [or sell himself,] unto thee; thou shalt not serve thyself with him with the service of a servant, (Hebrew,) 40. but as a hired servant [hireling] and as a sojourner he shall be with thee, and shall serve thee unto the year of Jubilee: 41. And then shall he depart from thee, both he and his children with him, and shall return unto his own family, and unto the possession of his fathers shall he return. 42. For they are my servants, which I brought forth out of the land of Egypt: they shall not be sold with the sale of a servant (Hebrew). 43. Thou shalt not rule over him with rigor; but shalt fear thy God."

Observe, in regard to this statute, that it refers definitely and exclusively to the poor man who should find it difficult to sustain himself and his family, though not disabled, and who should choose to "sell himself" to his neighbor, to be his servant, for the purpose of bettering his circumstances. Any Jew, from the king on the throne to the meanest subject, might "sell himself," after the Jewish manner of "selling," to his neighbor, to be his servant, who should choose to do so. In none of the forms of Hebrew servitude was there the least oppression, injustice, unrighteousness, or impropriety. Any man might, if he chose, be a hired servant, a six years' servant, or a forever servant.

In the case of the poor man, referred to in the

statute before us, who, instead of maintaining his own home and engaging as a *hired servant*, should prefer to unite himself to his neighbor's household after the manner of the common six years' servant, some special regulations would be needed. "Thou shalt not serve thyself with him with the service of a servant, [common six years' servant,] but as a hired servant, [hireling,] and as a sojourner he shall be with thee." That is, although, to relieve his poverty, he should sell himself, and receive the pay in advance, just as did the common, or six years' servant, yet his relation to the household should be altogether temporary, and only like that of the hired servant, or sojourner. His own household should not be broken up and merged in that of his employer, as was the case with the common, or six years' servant. It would manifestly be very trying, and oppressive even, for a man, on account of poverty, to break up his own household and incorporate himself into his neighbor's household, like a six years' servant. This, therefore, was kindly forbidden. His own family standing should remain, though he was joined, for the time being, with another family. He should still be recognized as a separate household, in the observance of the Passover and other religious feasts, and in his standing as a Hebrew citizen.

Again, such a state of dependence as this would need to come to an end at the sounding of the Jubilee trumpet.—V. 40, 41. In order to the best and happiest observance of the great sabbatic year of Jubilee, the man and his family should resume their standing as an independent household. The presumption and expectation in such cases would be, that the assistance derived from this temporary service to his neighbor would enable him to sustain himself, and maintain this standing afterward. This "selling of himself" to his neighbor for the time being, was simply the resort of a poor man, able to work, and thus help himself, in order to better his circumstances. Such cases would occur, of course, as they do among all peoples, in all ages. This statute was designed to restrict such arrangements, and prevent their breaking up the household, a most sacred thing in the Mosaic economy. "And shall return unto his own family, and unto the possession of his fathers shall he return, both he and his children with him."

Notice further, in regard to this statute, that the idea of "bondage," which crops out in our English translation of the 39th verse, "Thou shalt not compel him to serve as a bond-servant," is altogether a gloss of the translators. The Hebrew yields no such idea. The word translated "bond-servant" is the common word for servant, and the same word that is used to designate Hebrew servants in Ex. xxi: 2–6. The contrast in this statute is not at all between Jews and Gentile, but between the common servant and the hired servant. This is expressly stated in verses 39 and 40. Neither of these classes of servants were bond-servants in any degraded or oppressive sense.

Observe, too, that this statute throughout relates to a particular class of persons. It is manifest, from the allusion to the "stranger" and "sojourner," in the 35th verse of this chapter, that the persons referred to might be either Jews or Gentiles. It is the particular case of the poor man with his family, Jew or Gentile, who should seek to better his circumstances by "selling himself" (in the Hebrew sense) to his neighbor.

From overlooking this obvious fact, some have supposed that this statute contains a general prohibition against making servants of Jews. But this supposition is in flat contradiction to the statute in Ex. xxi: 2–7, and, therefore, can not be admitted. And this statute does not even pretend to forbid any such thing. It simply commands that the poor *neighbor* ("And if thy brother that *dwelleth by thee* be waxen poor,") who should sell himself, should not be merged in the household like the six years' servant, but should sustain only a temporary relation thereto, like the hired servant. This statute is just as applicable to people of foreign blood as to native Hebrews.

This statute also closes with a beautiful allusion to the deliverance from Egypt. "For they are my servants which I brought forth out of the land of Egypt: they shall not sell themselves with the sale of a servant." (Hebrew.) These poor, unfortunate families are just as much the servants of God as the rich: really on a perfect level with them, as God's children: as such they should be regarded and treated: in their peculiar circumstances, they should not be held and considered as common six years' servants: their household should not be extinguished: they should go out at the Jubilee to return to their own home and paternal estate: and as an independent household in Israel should they serve the Lord, whose servants they were as much as any in Israel. All the people were commanded not to abuse such poor, dependent families, but to fear God in reference to them.—V. 43.

This, then, is not a statute concerning the Jubilee. It refers to the Jubilee only incidentally. It is a statute of special protection to a particular class of poor people, who, in their peculiar circumstances, might be liable to abuse. The idea of slavery, either as it respects Jews or Gentiles, is not in it.

Statute concerning Foreign Servants.

We come now, next in order, to the very innocent, but quite famous, statute concerning foreign servants. This, as it stands in our English translation, is as follows: v. 44–46. 44. "Both thy bondmen, and thy bondmaids, which thou shalt have, shall be of the heathen that are round about you: of them shall ye buy bondmen and bondmaids. 45. Moreover, of the children of the strangers that do sojourn among you, of them shall ye buy, and of their families that are with you, which they begat in your land: and they shall be your possession. 46. And ye shall take them as an inheritance for

your children after you, to inherit them for a possession; they shall be your bondmen forever."

Now, taking this as a distinct and separate section
in this message from the Lord to the children of
Israel comprised in these two chapters, we invite
attention to the following observations concerning it.

1. The idea of "bondage," which the translators,
designedly or undesignedly, have apparently diffused
so freely through this whole passage, really does not
appear in the Hebrew. There is no different word
used from that which is usually used to designate
servants, either Jews or Gentiles. Any schoolboy
that can read Hebrew, can see this, by examining
the passage in the original. We have noticed this
fact before.

2. The passage stands in no position of contrast
either with what precedes it, or with what comes
after it. The notion that it stands in contrast with
the preceding statute in such a sense that we are
to understand, from the two together, that Jews
might not be held as "bondmen," while Gentiles
might, is altogether a myth. Nothing is really said
about "bondmen" in either passage. As Judge Jay
has well remarked, the word "bondmen," in this
passage, is "comment," and not translation. Such
contrast, furthermore, is impossible, from the fact
that the preceding statute is not concerning the
Jews generally, but concerning a particular class of
Jews, and probably itself includes Gentiles of the
same class.

Nor again, is the assumption that the preceding

statute commanded that Jewish servants should go out at the Jubilee, while this directed that foreign servants should be held as "bondmen *forever*," any better. There is no such contrast between the two passages as to afford the least ground for such assumption. This statute in regard to foreign servants contains no allusion to the Jubilee whatever. It is no part of the Jubilee statute. It is a statute by itself, like others both before and after it. The particular class of servants referred to in the preceding statute, were to go out at the Jubilee, whether Jews or Gentiles: in this statute nothing is said, one way or the other, as to the going out of the Gentile servants spoken of.

3. It should be noticed further, that, really, this is not properly a statute concerning foreign servants, but simply a *grant of permission* to the Jews to have such servants. It lays down no rules for the treatment of such servants, and none for their own behavior. The only thing in it is permission to the Jews to have foreign servants. It contains no hint whether they were to have them as hired servants, or six years' servants, or continuously permanent servants.

All this will be still more manifest when the passage is divested of the mistaken coloring which our English translation gives it. The following translation of the whole passage is from the pen of a Hebrew scholar, whose candor, learning, and good judgment no one will be disposed to dispute.*

* Rev. J. Morgan, D. D.

13

"Thy servant and thy handmaid which shall be to thee
from the nations which are round about you,—from them ye
shall acquire servant and handmaid: and also from the sons
of the inhabitants which sojourn with you, from them ye
shall acquire, and from their families which are with you,
which they have begotten in your land; and they shall be to
you for a possession; and ye shall inherit them for your-
selves and your children after you to possess (as) a possession: forever in, or by, them shall ye serve."

This translation is very literal and idiomatic, but
faithful to the original, inspired Hebrew. The one
single thing in this message from the Lord is simple permission to the Jews to have, or "possess,"
foreign servants, either from the nations around
them, or from foreign families dwelling among them.
This grant was to be continuous, "forever." The
servants are designated by precisely the same terms
as are usually used to designate Hebrew servants,
and not a word is said as to the position these foreign servants were to occupy, or how they were to
be treated, or how the servants themselves should
demean themselves. It really has nothing to do with
the Jubilee, and stands in no such relation to other
statutes as to give it a special signification.

In what sense the Jews were thus permitted to
"possess" foreign servants as "a possession," may
be learned from a parallel passage in Isa. xiv: 1, 2:
"For the Lord will have mercy on Jacob, and will
yet choose Israel, and set them in their own land:
and the strangers shall be joined with them, and
they shall cleave to the house of Jacob. And the

people shall take them, and bring them to their place: and the house of Israel shall possess them in the land of the Lord for servants and handmaids: and they shall take them captives, whose captives they were; and they shall rule over their oppressors." Barnes says, that by the term "strangers," we are to understand "those foreigners who would become proselytes to their [the Jewish] religion while they were in Babylon." These "strangers" would "join" themselves to the Jews, as the people of God, though in captivity, much as young converts join a Christian church: and the Jews would "take them" and "possess them for servants and handmaids," much as Christian churches take converts and possess them for servants and handmaids. Yet these "strangers" were foreigners, and would be, as members of Jewish households, foreign servants. They would be to the Jews for a possession forever: that is, they would be permanently united to them, to be one people with them, and belong to them as part and parcel of them. In like manner the Jews were permitted, by this grant in this passage in Leviticus, to procure and possess foreign servants both from the nations around them, and from families dwelling among them. There would be no ceremonial contamination in this, and no disturbance of God's plan in reference to the Jews as a separate people. It would really be helping to accomplish the great object God had in view in all this plan, namely, the salvation of the souls of men.

The inquiry now arises, How foreign servants, admitted to Jewish households, were to be treated, and under what regulations they were to come?

We have already seen that, in the grant permitting the Jews to have foreign servants, there is not even a hint in answer to these inquiries. We shall also find, on investigation, that specific rules and regulations in regard to foreign servants are nowhere else to be found in the Mosaic code.

Now, this entire absence of all laws for the regulation of foreign servants, in the Mosaic code, points to the true answer to the foregoing inquiries. As *servants,* they were to come under the same rules and regulations as were Jewish servants. Specific and very definite rules were given concerning Jewish servants of all classes: if foreign servants were to come under the same rules, plainly nothing further was needed. If they were to come under different regulations, surely such regulations would have been given. The undeniable fact that no such regulations are to be found in the Mosaic code, makes it safe for us to conclude that foreign servants were to come under the same rules and regulations as were Jewish servants.

This is confirmed by the frequent announcement, in the Mosaic code, of the principle that strangers and native Jews were to be under the same laws. "Ye shall have one manner of law, as well for the stranger, as for one of your own country: for I am the Lord your God."—Lev. xxiv: 22. "But the stranger that dwelleth with you shall be unto you as one born among you, and thou shalt love him as thyself: for ye were strangers in the land of Egypt; I am the Lord your God."—Lev. xix: 34. "Also thou shalt not oppress a stranger, for ye know the heart of a stranger, seeing ye were strangers in the land of Egypt."—Ex. xxiii: 9. Verily, if the Jews were permitted to admit the stranger, or foreigner, into their households, they were well and most impressively instructed how to regard him and treat him. "Thou shall love him as thyself." This is the uniform teaching of the Mosaic code. There was no need that any Jew should misunderstand it. No warrant can be found in the Mosaic code for oppressing or degrading the stranger.

It is, indeed, true that foreign servants, *as foreigners*, and because they were foreigners, were somewhat restricted as to certain privileges, as were foreigners who were not servants. But the evidence can not be found that the Mosaic code designed to degrade them, or restrict their privileges in the least *as* foreign *servants*, and because they were foreign servants. As servants, they were to be regarded and treated, in all respects, as were Jewish servants. As foreigners, they were to come under the same laws as were other foreigners.

If the Jewish Talmuds, or the traditions of the elders, did pretend to teach that the Jews were "forbidden to tyrannize over their own countrymen," while it was "lawful to make a Canaanitish servant serve with rigor," as some commentators tell us, we protest that no such teaching as this is found in the law of Moses. It is flatly contradicted by the passages which we have quoted. Mere inferences are not to be exalted above the express declarations of the Divine Word. We believe in Moses, but we do not believe in Talmuds, and traditions, and false interpretations.

Resuming our analysis of the chapter, we come next, as sustaining some natural relation to the preceding statute giving permission to the Jews to have foreign servants, which we have just examined, to the statute concerning Jewish servants whose _masters were foreigners_. This occupies the rest of the chapter, beginning, as we suppose, at the middle of the 46th verse. The division of the Bible into chapters and verses is a modern invention, and is of no account, except that it not unfrequently misleads the reader. We think there should be a period at the word "forever," in the 46th verse, and that that is the conclusion of the statute in regard to foreign servants, and that the rest of the verse belongs to the following statute. Our reasons for this will be stated very briefly.

The word "but," in our English translation, which expresses opposition and connection between the two parts of the verse, is merely a comment of the translators. The Hebrew word which is here rendered "but," is, in all respects, the identical word that is usually translated _and_. Says Judge Jay: "The initial use of _and_ is a peculiarity of the Hebrew, and especially of the style of Moses. Of the one hundred and eighty-seven chapters composing the Pentateuch, no less than one hundred and twenty-eight commence with *and*. Even the *books* of Leviticus and Numbers thus begin. Innumerable are the laws and precepts prefaced with *and*."* If, therefore, we substitute *and* for *but*, our translation of this verse will be much more faithful to the inspired Hebrew.

Supposing now, that the statute concerning the employment of foreign servants ends with the word " forever" in the 46th verse, the next statute, which occupies the remainder of the chapter, will begin as follows: 46. "And over your brethren the children of Israel, ye shall not rule one over another with rigor. 47. And if a sojourner or stranger wax rich by thee, and thy brother that dwelleth by him wax poor, and sell himself unto the stranger or sojourner by thee, or to the stock of the stranger's family, after that he is sold he may be redeemed." There is some natural connection between the injunction, " And over your brethren the children of Israel, ye shall not rule one over another with rigor," and the statute which follows, as may be seen by referring to the conclusion of the statute, " And the other shall not rule with rigor over him in thy sight."—V. 53. As if it had been said, " Ye shall not rule over your brethren of the children of Israel with rigor," neither "shall ye permit the stranger or the sojourner to rule over them with rigor," as he might be disposed to do in this particular case of a poor Jew sold to him to be his servant. We think, therefore, that the latter part of the 46th verse has a more

* Mosaic Laws of Servitude, p. 44.

natural connection with what follows it than with what precedes it. It undoubtedly has a general and indirect connection with most of the statutes that precede it in the chapter : but to give it a close disjunctive connection with the statute concerning foreign servants, so as to make the whole mean that Jews should not rule with rigor over their brethren of the children of Israel, while they might thus rule over foreign servants, we think absurd, and flatly contradictory to express declarations of Mosaic law.

This last section of this chapter, verses 46–55, is manifestly a statute concerning poor Jews with homes and families, who might have rich neighbors of foreign blood, to whom they should find it to their advantage to "sell themselves." It was perfectly proper, so far as appears, for Jews to sell themselves thus to foreigners to be their servants, if they were so disposed. This statute contemplated such cases, and is a statute for the protection of the servant and his family from abuse. In the first place, it especially encouraged redemption.—Verses 48–52. In the next place, this statute provided, of course, that the servant should be regarded only as "a yearly hired servant."—V. 53. The poor Jew thus "sold" to his neighbor Gentile should not lose his own family standing, any more than the poor Jew who was sold to his neighbor Jew, as provided for in verses 39–43. He could sustain to the family of his employer only the relation of "a hired servant," notwithstanding he had "sold himself" as the six years' servants did, and as the hired servants never did. Finally, "he and his children" should "go out in the year of Jubilee," and return to their home and possessions. These regulations would sufficiently guard this particular class of poor Jewish families, when adverse circumstances compelled them to engage ·as servants to their rich Gentile neighbors. Neither Jewish masters nor Gentile masters should rule over them with rigor.

Next in order in this message from the Lord to the children of Israel, chapter xxvi: 1, is a statute ' concerning *idolatry*. Following this, verse 2, is a command respecting "Sabbaths." The next section, verses 3–13, pronounces the richest blessings upon obedience : and the concluding section of the message, verses 14–45, details the most terrible curses upon disobedience.

1. Now, in all these rules and regulations in regard to servants and others contained in this remarkable passage of Scripture, we have found neither slaves nor chattel slavery: no, not so much even as a hint at any thing of the sort. The legislation therein is all concerning servants, and none of it concerning slaves.

2. We have found no degradation or oppression of foreign servants. Warrant for such degradation can not be found in the Pentateuch.

3. We have found no degradation or oppression of servants of any sort. Such degradation can not be found in the laws of Moses.

4. We have found the most careful, kindly, and

benevolent provisions for the protection of servants and others, whose peculiar circumstances might render them liable to abuse.

5. In our judgment, the grant to the Jews to have foreign servants, never contemplated their going abroad to procure them. We think this grant extended, in general, only to such foreign servants as might come among the Jews from the nations around them: and also to the children of foreigners dwelling among them. Such foreigners might be taken into Jewish households as servants. They would thus be provided with homes, and brought under the influence of the true religion. This, as we understand it, was the object of this statute in regard to foreign servants. It was designed to absorb and make Jewish whatever foreign element might find its way into the Hebrew nation. It was one leading aim of the Mosaic code to keep the Jews a separate people, and it never could have designed to send the Jews abroad to bring in foreign elements. This would have been a fatal mistake, as might be abundantly shown.

But whatever foreign element should "be to them," would need some special provisions, in order that it might be absorbed and become Jewish. Foreigners settled in the land, and having homes of their own, might be circumcised and admitted to the privileges of the Jewish religion. Others might be admitted to Jewish households as servants, and so find homes, and be brought under Jewish influences. Precisely in harmony with all this was the statute in regard to fugitive servants. "Thou shalt not deliver unto his master the servant which is escaped from his master unto thee: He shall dwell with thee, even among you, in that place which he shall choose in one of thy gates where it liketh him best: thou shalt not oppress him."—Deut. xxiii: 15, 16. This undoubtedly refers to foreign servants escaping into the land of Judea. Such should be received with kindness, and permitted to use their own liberty in finding a dwelling-place where it should please them best. If they should come into the land of the Jews, they should be treated with justice and good will. But nowhere in the Mosaic code is there a hint that the Jews were expected to go abroad after foreign servants.

Finally, we regard this legislation in regard to foreign servants, in its true spirit, as a beautiful exemplification of the manner in which the Bible everywhere demands that all men shall remember the "brotherly covenant" which exists between man and man as members of the great brotherhood of the race. Instead of being a slave-catching statute, it is a statute of brotherly love. The Jews, for wise reasons, were to be, and to be kept, separate from all other peoples; nevertheless, whatever foreigners should find their way into the nation, were to be received into their households as readily as people of their own nation, and, with a few needful restrictions, were to be under the same laws and regulations. They were to be welcomed, and employed, and treated with that good will which the law of God requires. The express injunctions were:

" Ye shall have one manner of law, as well for the stranger as for one of your own country, for I am the Lord." "*Thou shalt love him as thyself.*" Love him by receiving him into their houses, giving him place and employment there, and, consequently, instruction in the true religion, for the everlasting salvation of his soul. And when he should be settled in the land and become rich, they should regard it as no degradation to find a home for the time being, and employment in his household.— Lev. xxv: 47. "The brotherly covenant" should be sacredly observed between them. Neither should "oppress" the other. If either thought of making merchandise of the other, the penalty of death, with the terrible thunder of Jehovah's voice in it, warned him to beware.

CHAPTER XV.

THE JEWISH FAMILY THE TRUE MODEL.

PROBABLY the Abrahamic household, somewhat restricted and limited by the Mosaic legislation, was the true model of the family. Our modern arrangements in regard to the family are somewhat too limited. There is a large class of isolated, half-vagabond people, that might be made a blessing to themselves, and to others, if they could, in some way, be incorporated into the family. As it is, their life is a cheerless, unsocial, profitless one. This is deeply felt both in America and in Europe; and various experiments have been made, and expedients resorted to, to remedy this evil, but with very poor success, for the most part. A little enlargement of the modern household, both in benevolence and dimensions, like the Jewish household under the Mosaic restrictions, would exactly meet the difficulty, and, doubtless, be an improvement upon modern society. This is not *socialism*, nor any thing like it. It is the golden mean between the narrowest household of the hermit, and the broad and unmanageable system of modern socialism. It preserves the family intact and pure, and, at the same time, furnishes a real home for the poor and homeless.

There was no poor-house in Palestine : there was no need of any. The semi-Patriarchal household supplied its place, and was much better. But how monstrous the perversion which has turned this most beautiful, and most benevolent, and wisest household arrangement which the world ever saw, into the villainous system of chattel slavery ! *O tempora ! O mores !*

CHAPTER XVI.

NEW TESTAMENT TEACHING CONCERNING SERVITUDE.

The writers of the New Testament Jews—Hebrew and not Greek writers—True method of understanding any Language—New Testament usage main guide in interpreting New Testament Language—Mistake of Conybeare and How-son—Classic meaning of δοῦλος—New Testament usage of δοῦλος—Inferences and Conclusions.

IT is impossible rightly to understand any ancient writings or documents, without taking into account the character and circumstances of the writers. Let us remember, then, that the writers of the New Testament were Jews, and, as writers, had the character of Jews. All their previous education and training were Jewish, and not Grecian nor Roman. Their ideas, feelings, and modes of thought were thoroughly Jewish. They were bred in the Hebrew family: indoctrinated in Hebrew law and religion. They wrote as Jews: they did not write either as Greeks or Romans. The fact that they used the Greek language does not militate against these statements at all. They wrote in the Greek language, because, in the providence of God, that was the common language of Western Asia at the time, and because it was the best language in which to have such inspired writings as theirs were, preserved to the world. They were not, properly speaking, Greek writers, but Jewish writers using the Greek language. This is an all-important fact, to be understood and remembered. Says Dr. Robinson, in his preface to his Lexicon of the New Testament: "The writers of the New Testament applied the Greek language to subjects on which it had never been employed by native Greek writers. No native Greek had ever written on Jewish affairs, nor on the Jewish theology and ritual. Hence the seventy, in their translation, had often to employ Greek words as the signs of things and ideas which heretofore had been expressed only in Hebrew. In such a case, *they could only select those Greek words which most nearly corresponded to the Hebrew; leaving the different shade or degree of signification to be gathered by the reader from the context.*" "Thus far the path was indeed already broken for the writers of the New Testament. But beyond this, they were to be the instruments of making known a new revelation, a new dispensation of mercy to mankind. Here was opened a wide circle of new ideas, and new doctrines to be developed, for which all human language was as yet too poor; and this poverty was to be done away, even as at the present day, on the discovery and culture of a new science, *chiefly by enlarging the signification and application of words already in use, rather than by the formation of new ones.*" "The New Testament, then, was written by Hebrews, aiming to express Hebrew thoughts, conceptions, feelings, in the Greek tongue. Their idiom, consequently, in soul and spirit, is Hebrew; in its external form, Greek, and that more or less pure, according to the facilities which an individual writer may have possessed for acquiring fluency and accuracy of expression in that tongue."

No scholar will question the correctness of these views. In the progress of all languages, various words, more or less numerous, vary or change their meanings, to a greater or less extent. In the transfer of words from one language to another, there will often be still greater changes in the meaning of the words so transferred. Words, for example, introduced from foreign languages into the English, very generally have to be Anglicised to suit English mind and English modes of thought. The only proper method of ascertaining the true meaning of such words in the English language, is to study their *present usage in that language.* A departure from this rule would lead to the grossest errors. Something indeed can be learned in regard to the force and meaning of words introduced into our language from foreign tongues, by studying both their primitive and derived meanings in those tongues from which they are transferred; yet to ascertain their exact shades of meaning, as now used in English, their present usage in the English must be studied. No man of sense ever thinks of disregarding this rule. No man of sense and of learning ever thinks of going to Cicero to learn what our Anglo-Latin word *"auspices"* now means. The Latin correspondent of this word was a favorite word with the great Roman orator, but in a

14

sense much different from that in which it is now used in English composition. It has been Anglicised to meet and suit English mind and English modes of thought.

This rule has a large, special, and important application to the Greek of the New Testament. The Greek language of the New Testament is heathen, Attic Greek, Hebraized to meet and suit Christianized Hebrew mind and modes of thought. To understand it we need, to be sure, a knowledge of classic Greek, but we need more a thorough knowledge of Hebrew mind and thought, and of Christian ideas and experiences. We need to study the language of the New Testament in the light of the New Testament, and of the Old Testament, in order to understand it. Heathen classic usage can never fully and properly expound for us the sense of the New Testament.

Hence, most manifestly, the scope and teachings of the New Testament in regard to the particular subject of servitude, can never be properly understood simply by a study of old Grecian and Roman customs, and the usages of words in ancient Grecian literature. These may furnish some help, but they by no means constitute the standard of interpretation. To make them the standard would lead to the grossest errors. As a representative example of this sort of mistake, we have a notable instance in Conybeare and Howson's translation of Paul's Epistles. Those learned authors have undertaken to translate the New Testament word, δοῦλος, by the English word "*slave*," or "bondsman" in the sense of slave. This is both a classical and a hermeneutical blunder. The English word "*slave*" is very considerably narrower in signification than even the classical usage of the Greek word δοῦλος. It often refers, in classic Greek, to servants that are not slaves: to unchattelized, free servants.* It quite commonly, to be sure, refers to *slaves*, but it frequently has a wider sense, referring to servants that are not slaves. So that it is an abuse even of classical usage to restrict this word, in any author, to the exclusive, specific sense of "*slave*," and obstinately attach this particular sense to the word wherever found, without regard to the character, subject, or scope of the author. Simple classic usage, therefore, should have taught these learned authors better than to make Paul call himself the "bondsman," or "*slave*" of the Lord Jesus Christ, as they have very foolishly done in several instances. We strongly opine that the Good Shepherd does

---

* Many writers have been misled by the frequent *application* of the word δοῦλος, in classic Greek, to *slaves*, and so have mistaken its true sense. In a slaveholding community the general word for *servant* will often be applied to slaves. Slaves are servants: or rather they are both servants and slaves. Hence the Greeks, among whom slavery existed, applied the general term δοῦλος to their slaves. The general sense, however, often appears in classic usage, though the term is freely *applied* to slaves. But this frequent application of the term to slaves, is not the least indication that the word is not properly a general term. Our English word *servant* is very much applied to slaves in our Southern states; but for all that, the word properly means *servant*, in the general sense, and would, if slaves existed wherever the English language is known, and this word was everywhere much applied to them. So of δοῦλος. Its proper sense, as a general term, is not disturbed in the least by its frequent application, by the slaveholding Greeks, to their slaves. Its primary, general sense frequently crops out in classic usage. "Apud Xenoph. Anab. . . . . satrapa regius δοῦλος vocatur."—*Schleusner.*

not care to be announced in this world as the great slaveholder of the universe! Even classic usage does not quite necessitate this. To take one particular application of a word, and restrict its usage and meaning exclusively and specifically to that, is very unclassic indeed. To do this with the Greek word δοῦλος, as used in the New Testament, is manufacturing gospel-slaveholding at a rapid rate truly. If these gentlemen were not Englishmen, we should be tempted to suspect *cotton* somewhere.

In the second place, the word δοῦλος has figurative and other uses in the New Testament which utterly forbid the notion that it was used by the sacred writers as a specific term for "*slave:*" uses which the word "*slave,*" in its modern sense, never does have and never could have.

Before referring to particular passages, we wish to remind the reader of the fact that this word is of very frequent occurrence in the New Testament. It occurs at least one hundred and twenty-five times. If it should be translated *slave* in every instance, we verily believe it would frighten the most hardy translator and the most stolid reader. Such a translation would fill the New Testament with discourse about slaves, and people the land of Judea, in Apostolic times, thick with slaves, whereas the truth is, as Dr. Kitto and other biblical scholars affirm, there were neither slaves nor slavery there at the time.

In referring to passages to exhibit the New Testament usage of the word δοῦλος, *doulos*, we will take the first example of its use that occurs in each book of the New Testament, until we have gone as far as the patience of the reader will permit. Matt. viii: 9—"For I am a man under authority, having soldiers under me: and I say to this man, go, and he goeth; and to another, come, and he cometh; and to my '*servant*,' do this, and he doeth it." The use of the word in such a passage as this determines nothing one way or another. The "*servant*" alluded to may have been a free servant, or a slave servant, for aught the passage itself shows: so we will leave it. The word in question, however, is used thirty times in the book of Matthew, rightly translated *servant*, in the general sense. In several of these places, to translate it *slave*, is wholly inadmissible. But we will pass on, confining ourselves to the first example in each book, in order that the reader may not accuse us of unfairness. Mark. x: 44—"And whosoever of you will be the chiefest, shall be '*servant*' of all." This was spoken especially to the apostles, after the two sons of Zebedee, James and John, had made request of Jesus that they might sit, one on his right hand and the other on his left hand in his glory. Let us put in the word *slave*, instead of the word "*servant*," and see how it will then read, which will give us exactly the right sense, if δοῦλος, *doulos*, is the specific term for slave, and properly means *slave*. "And whosoever of you will be the chiefest, shall be '*slave*' of all." This makes either supreme nonsense, or sense supremely base. Slave service, and the service of love and good-will referred to in this passage, are totally different. In no sense is he that renders the latter a slave. Of all persons he is furthest removed from slavery. It is infinitely absurd to use the word slave in any such sense. And where, in all the usage of language in modern times, can we find a similar example? Such a usage is preposterous and unnatural. We never meet with it. The free service of love and good-will, such as the law of God requires, makes any man who renders it *"chiefest"* of all. This is the noblest service that can be rendered, and makes any man who renders it the noblest *"servant"*—a royal *"servant"* in God's moral kingdom. But it is simply supremely ridiculous to call such an individual a *slave*.

The first example in Luke is found, ii : 29—"Lord, now lettest thou thy *'servant'* depart in peace, according to thy word." These are the words of Simeon, spoken in the temple, when he took the child Jesus up in his arms, and blessed God that his eyes had been permitted to see the great salvation. Was Simeon, then, one of God's old *slaves?* Does the word *slave* give us a right idea of his character and relations to God? Is there a peculiar fitness in speaking of him as God's old *slave?* If δοῦλος, *doulos,* meant slave, these questions must be answered in the affirmative. The absurdity of this is sufficiently apparent. But let us pass on. John iv: 51—"And as he was now going down, his *'servants'* met him, and told him, saying, Thy son liveth." There is surely nothing here to prove that the word means *slave*. Acts ii: 18—"And on my '*servants*' and on my hand-maidens I will pour out in those days of my Spirit; and they shall prophesy." Here again, if the word translated "*servants*" meant slaves, we have God set forth as a slaveholder. In what community on the face of the earth is it natural and edifying to Christian people either to speak or think of God, the great Father, in this light? The word "*servant*," in its freest and best sense, exactly gives the meaning: the word slave gives a sense that is sufficiently shocking. Rom. i: 1—"Paul, a servant of Jesus Christ, called to be an apostle." Paul a *slave* of Jesus Christ. But Christ took upon himself the form of a δοῦλος, *doulos*, "*slave*." Paul, then, was the slave of the slave Jesus Christ. All this is perfectly fit, and nicely rhetorical and beautiful, if *slave* is the true meaning of the word. 1 Cor. vii: 21—"Art thou called being a '*servant?*' care not for it." Whether a chattelized or an unchattelized servant, of course this passage does not necessarily teach. If, however, "*servant*" means slave, then we venture to affirm that the direction which follows is one which it is impossible to obey. No man, in his senses, can be a chattel slave and not care for it. The command is a good deal more than human nature, or rather the human soul, can bear. The poor slave may be able to endure his wrongful bondage patiently, but to command him "not to care for it" is commanding more than he can perform, until his manhood is all whipped and crushed out of him. We can never believe that God ever laid such a command upon the suffering and robbed slave. 2 Cor. iv: 5—"For we preach not ourselves, but Christ Jesus the Lord; and ourselves your '*servants*' for Jesus' sake." We do not believe that Paul ever designed to call himself the *slave* of any man or men. He was, above all others, next to his Divine Master, the "*servant*" of all, to render to them the cordial service of love and .good-will: but he was no man's *slave*.

We will pursue these quotations no further. These examples may be taken as fair specimens of the manner in which this word, δοῦλος, *doulos*, is used in the New Testament. John, the Revelator, applies this same word to himself, to the prophets, to Moses, and to the inhabitants of heaven. How incongruous and preposterous to make such an application of the word "*slave!*" In multitudes of passages in the New Testament, to translate δοῦλος, *doulos*, by our word *slave*, makes the most consummate nonsense. We do not believe that there is a single instance of its use in the New Testament that will bear this translation. This word is rightly translated by our general term "*servant,*" in its free sense, or in its most general sense.*

---

* We have not room to multiply authorities: and should not have extended this discussion to such length, if some very modern translators and interpreters had not made apparently desperate efforts to limit the word δοῦλος, in the New Testament, to the specific sense of *slave*. But we can not forbear quoting the following from Schleusner, in regard to the meaning of this word in the Greek Scriptures:

"Apud Graecos Scriptt. latius interdum patet et omnino *eum* significat, *qui aliqua, quæcunque tandem sit, ratione alterius imperio subest.*"—Lex. Graeco-Latinum in Novum Testamentum: Art. δοῦλος. The substance of this is, that this

As this is the only word which is often translated *"servant"* in the New Testament, and the only word to which the sense *slave* can, with any show of reason, be attached, we wish to present other considerations to confirm the statement just made.

1. In the first place, then, let it be again distinctly noted that, in the Greek language the word δοῦλος, *doulos*, is a general, and not a specific term. Says Dr. Albert Barnes: "The Greeks used the term δοῦλος, *doulos*, to express servitude *in the most general form*, whatever might be the method by which the obligation to service originated." This is, unquestionably, the character and usage of the word in the Greek language. In connection with this, let it also be remembered that the Greek had another word which was the proper and specific word for *slave*. "The proper word to denote a slave, with reference to the master's right of property in him, and without regard to the relations and offices in which he was employed, was not δοῦλος, *doulos*, but ἀνδράποδον, *andrapodon*." "They," the Greeks, "used" this latter term "to denote *a slave* regarded as property."—*Dr. Barnes*. The Greek language, then, furnished the writers of the New Testament with the general term, δοῦλος, *doulos*, having precisely the sense of our English word *"servant,"* in its general signification; and with the specific term ἀνδράποδον, *andrapodon*, having the

word frequently has a wide signification in the Greek Scriptures, and signifies, in general, one who, for any reason whatever, is under the authority of another; that is, *servant*, in the general sense, as we have it in our English translation.

15

sense of our word "*slave*," in its specific sense. The two words were always at hand for use: one to mean "*servant*," in the general sense, and the other to mean "*slave*."

2. The law which should and would guide the writers of the New Testament in the use of these words, is manifest. That law is this: when they wished to give a specific sense, they would use the specific term; that is, they would use the word that means "*slave*," when that was simply and specific-ally the sense they wished to convey: when they wished to give a general sense, they would use the general term; that is, they would use the word that means "*servant*," in the general sense, when that was their meaning. The only exception to this rule is when the general term that means "*servant*" is so modified by the connection and other additional words as to necessitate the specific sense of "*slave*." When, therefore, the word δοῦλος, *doulos*, "serv-ant," is used in the New Testament, the general sense must always be understood, unless the con-nection and other words so modify the signification in a particular case as to necessitate a specific mean-ing. To illustrate: the word "*servant*," in English, unmodified, means *any servant*, or *servant in the general sense:* a chattelized servant, regarded and held as property, means a *slave*. The modifying words give the general term a specific sense. But where there are no modifying words and circum-stances, the general sense remains. Now, let the reader mark two facts. (1.) The specific and proper

word for *slave*, ἀνδράποδον, *andrapodon*, "*slave*,"
is never once used in the New Testament. It does
not belong to New Testament literature. There it
was, in the language, with just as much aptitude for
use, if needed, as δοῦλος, *doulos*, "*servant*." It was
always at hand, just as easy of use as the other, if
it had been wanted. It was not once wanted. If
the writers had wished to say *slave* in any instance,
here was the word for it. The inevitable conclusion
is, that in the cases where they use the word that
means "*servant*," they did not mean simply and
specifically, "*slave;*" or that they so modified and
restricted the general term "*servant*," as to give it
the specific sense of "*slave*." (2.) This leads us to
the other fact, namely, that in no case in the New
Testament is the word δοῦλος, *doulos*, "*servant*" so
modified as to necessitate the sense of *slave*. Being
a general term, it must be so modified by the connection and other words, in order to mean *slave*.
But in no case in the New Testament is it so modified. We have examined all the places where the
word occurs, and do not hesitate to make this statement. The passages in which there is the most
appearance of this will be examined in another
chapter. The conclusion, then, is inevitable and
irrefragable, that the word δοῦλος, *doulos*, "*servant*,"
never has the limited and specific sense of *slave*
in the New Testament.

3. In confirmation of all this, it may be observed
further, that this accords exactly with Hebrew mind
and usage. The writers of the New Testament,

with Jesus Christ, were Hebrews: christianized Hebrews, trained up and molded under the influence
of Hebrew ideas, modes of thought, and customs.
This fact, as forcibly stated in the quotation already
made from Dr. Robinson, had all to do with their
style of composition and use of the Greek language.
We have seen that, as a matter of fact, these writers
avoided the specific word in Greek which means
slave, and employed the general term which means
servant.   This is just what might have been expected
of such Hebrew writers.   As we have seen, slavery
never existed in the Hebrew nation: slaves were
never held there.   The Hebrew mind was not accustomed to either, and had no words for either.
It was accustomed to free servitude, and free servants of various classes: it had words for these.   It
had seen, from time to time, much oppression of
free servants, and was accustomed, both without and
with the inspiration of the Almighty, to denounce
such oppression.   Its Hebrew word for "servant,"
like our English word *servant*, was a general term
meaning any sort of servant.   The origin and history of the word, and the laws and usages of the
people, would always secure to this word a free
sense.   Now, in using the Greek language, in what
sense would Hebrew writers be likely to use a similar
and corresponding general term in that language?
But one answer can be given to this question.
Nothing could be more unnatural and absurd than
to suppose that they would use such a word as a
specific term for *slave*.   No similar instance of the

use of words can be found in the literature of the world. But nothing could be more natural than that they should employ the general Greek term δοῦλος, *doulos*, "*servant*," precisely as they had been accustomed to use the corresponding Hebrew term. This they have done.

4. One thing more. The word "*servant*," in a *free community* where slavery does not exist, usually refers in its usage to *free servants*. It is applied to all classes of servants that exist in that community. It is capable of a wider sense, to be sure, and may be extended to include all sorts of servants every-where. But common usage in a community where slavery does not exist, would apply the word to such servants as actually do exist there, that is, to all sorts of free servants, since slave servants are ex-cluded by the supposition. And this is the common use of the word "*servant*" in these Northern states, where slavery does not exist. The word is applied to any class of free servants; or, when extended in its signification and application, any servants what-ever. When individual servants, or classes of serv-ants are spoken of in a free community, it is under-stood that the servants are free servants. When the term is used in its widest and most general sense, as it often is, then the meaning is understood to be any servant or servants whatever. When a kitchen serv-ant is referred to, the assumption always is, in a free community, that that servant is a free servant: when a factory servant is referred to, the assumption is that that servant is a free servant. So generally.

When the word *"servant"* is used without qualification, and in the widest sense, then it means any sort of servant whatever. But the simple word *"servant,"* unqualified, never has the specific sense of *slave*, in a community where slavery does not exist. It may mean some particular, individual free servant, or any free servant whatever, or any servant whatever: but it never means specifically *a slave*.

Now, it is notorious that there was no slavery in Palestine in the time of Christ and when the New Testament was written. Christ lived and taught in a non-slaveholding community. The writers of the New Testament were brought up, and lived, and wrote in a non-slaveholding community. Their nation had always been a non-slaveholding nation. They had always, as native Hebrews, been accustomed to non-slaveholding and free society ideas and usages, and to the use of a general term, in the Hebrew language, precisely like our general word *"servant."* They found a corresponding word in the Greek language, and used it. The inference is irresistible that they would use that word, which is δοῦλος, *doulos*, first, in its proper sense as a general term, and secondly, in accordance with the ideas and usages of free society. This would entirely exclude from the word, in its simple and unmodified form, the specific sense of *slave*. When, therefore, the simple, unmodified term δοῦλος, *doulos*, *"servant"* occurs, we are to understand either any or *all classes of servants*, or *free servants*. By no legitimate possibility can we get any nearer the signification *slave*. The simple, unmodified term δοῦλος, *doulos*, "*servant*," can never mean *slave*, in the New Testament, without violating all rules of logic and sound interpretation. If it ever means *slave*, it must be because the connection and other qualifying words necessitate such meaning. Whether it is ever used in this way will be discussed in another chapter.

CHAPTER XVII.

EXPOSITION OF PASSAGES IN THE NEW TESTAMENT
WRITINGS WHICH SPEAK OF THE DUTIES OF
MASTERS.

Eph. vi : 9 ; *Col.* iv : 1.

Is the word δοῦλος, *servant*, ever so modified in
its use in the New Testament as necessarily to
restrict its meaning to the specific sense of *slave?*
We have demonstrated, in the preceding chapter,
that it must be so modified in order to have that
specific sense : is it so modified ?

1. If . it is so modified as necessarily to mean
slave, then we have the singular fact, that in every
case where the writers of the New Testament wished
to say *slave*, they, in every such instance, used a circumlocution with a multiplication of words to express
that sense, instead of using the single, specific word
in the Greek language which means *slave*. In
other words, we have the singular fact that all the
writers of the New Testament, when they wished
to say *slave*, ἀνδράποδον, *andrapodon*, always said
servant, δοῦλος, *doulos*, so modified as to limit its
signification to the sense of *slave*, that is, *slave
servant*. This certainly appears very unlikely.

2. In the second place, if *servant*, δοῦλος, *doulos*,
modified, is the uniform mode of saying *slave* in the

New Testament, the modifying words, adjuncts, and circumstances ought to be very definite and unequivocal. For δοῦλος, *doulos*, can not be uniformly translated *slave* in the New Testament without making the grossest nonsense in most of the places where it is used. If, therefore, in some few cases it really means *slave*, it ought to be, and would be, so modified as to make this sense unequivocal. For how else could it be known when it meant *slave*, and when it meant *servant*, in the general sense? We are to look, then, for a modification that shall be distinct and unequivocal, and that can not be mistaken.

3. It is, however, only by examining particular passages that we can determine whether the word *servant*, δοῦλος, *doulos*, is so modified as necessarily to limit its signification to the simple sense of *slave*. It would be needless to examine all the passages in the New Testament in which the word occurs, in reference to this question. We will take all the passages where directions and commands are given to *servants*, δοῦλοι, *douloi*, or to *masters*. These are really all the passages that relate to this discussion.

All these passages are found in the writings of Paul. Those which speak of the duties of masters are only two: Eph. vi: 9, and Col. iv: 1. Those which refer to the duties of servants are the five following: 1 Cor. vii: 20–24; Eph. vi: 5–8; Col. iii: 22–25; 1 Tim. vi: 1–5; Titus, ii: 9, 10. Let us quote and carefully examine each of these passages, and see, if we can, whether they are so modified that the servants spoken of therein are, of necessity, *slave-servants*, or rather servants who are also *slaves*, or, more correctly still, simply *slaves* without reference to the question of service at all. And while we are doing this, to save time and space, and to avoid repeating quotations, we wish also to give a general exposition of these several passages as we go along. These two things may be conducted together, and mutually assist each other.

First passage: Eph. vi: 9—"And, ye masters, do the same things unto them, forbearing threatening: knowing that your Master also is in heaven; neither is there respect of persons with him."

In this passage the word δοῦλος, *doulos*, "servant" does not occur. This word, however, is found in immediate connection, and the pronoun "*them*" refers back to this word in the preceding verses. Its meaning, of course, is to be ascertained by referring to its antecedent. This will be examined when we come to consider the verses in connection, as speaking of the duties of servants. There is nothing in this verse itself which can possibly modify the pronoun *them*, so as to limit and refer its signification to *slaves*, except the word *masters*. If the word *masters* means *slave-owning masters*, then the word *them*, as referring back to servants, means *slaves*. If "*masters*" in this verse means *slaveholders*, of course the servants belonging to them are *slaves*. But there is nothing in this word "*masters*" to indicate that it refers to slaveholding masters. The Greek word for *"masters,"* in this passage, is usually translated *"lord,"* in the New Testament. It is of very frequent occurrence, and is applied to Jesus Christ much more frequently than to any one else. Its proper sense is not *slaveholder*, by any means. It is applied to any individual who occupies a station of superintendance, control, or authority. It has no reference to property-ownership in those under control. It is a proper word for all sorts of servants to use in referring to and designating their masters. It is a suitable word to apply to all sorts of persons that have the control of others—to all sorts of masters. In the verse before us it undoubtedly means *masters in the general sense:* all sorts of masters; and has no special reference to slaveholders whatever. There is nothing, therefore, in this passage which necessitates its reference to slaves or slaveholders. There is absolutely nothing which looks particularly in that direction.

The other passage, addressed particularly to *masters*, and defining their duties, is found in Col. iv: 1. "Masters give unto your servants that which is just and equal; knowing that ye also have a Master in heaven."

The same word is used here to mean *"masters"* as in the other passage, quoted from Ephesians. This same word occurs also in the latter part of the verse. If *slaves* and *slaveholders* are meant here, it will exactly give the sense to substitute these words for the words *"servants"* and *"masters."* We shall then get the full import and beauty of the passage. "Slaveholders give unto your slaves that which is just and equal: knowing that ye also have a slave-holder in heaven." The truth is, the word "*mas-ters*," as already shown, does not mean slave-owning masters specifically. The word "*servants*" is un-modified, and, consequently, can not have the specific sense of *slave*.

There is, therefore, absolutely nothing at all in either of these passages to necessitate or demand a particular reference to slaves and slaveholders. In neither of them are the terms used so modified as to indicate such reference. And, let it be remembered, there is not the least authority for giving them such reference without such modification.

To confirm all this, it may be remarked further, (1.) That so discriminating a writer as Paul would be very likely to say *slaves* and *slaveholders*, in some way very distinctly, if he meant exactly that and nothing else. He knew the difference well between general and specific statements, and knew very well how to make both very clearly. As a matter of fact, he has used only general terms unqualified, and it is altogether proper to conclude that his sense is general. If he had meant any particular sort of masters, in these passages, he was abundantly com-petent to say so. That he was not afraid to say so, is abundantly proved, from the fact that he has catalogued "*men-stealers*," in his First Epistle to Timo-thy, with "liars," "whore-mongers," and "murder-ers," for whom the law of God was especially made.

(2.) The view which we take is further confirmed by the consideration, that, if these ʼtwo passages under examination, which speak of the duties of masters, refer specifically to that particular class of masters who are slaveholders, then, in all Paul's writings, and in all the New Testament, we have not one solitary direction, or command, or exhortation, or instruction, addressed to any other sort or sorts of masters. Who believes that such a writer as Paul would single out slaveholding masters and give directions and commands to them, and leave all other masters wholly out of the account? Who believes that the teachings of the entire New Testament wholly pass by all masters, except slaveholders? But so it is, if these two passages refer specifically to slaveholders. The truth of the matter is, the language of these passages is general, and the sense is general. They refer to masters in the general sense, and are limited to no one class in particular.

(3.) One thing more. These directions, manifestly, assume the continuance of the relation involved in the terms *servant* and *master*. If these terms mean *slave* and *slaveholder*, then the relation is that of *slave* and *owner*. Now, mark: these directions are totally impossible to that relation. They can not be applied to it without annihilating it, any more than you can apply the Sermon on the Mount to the libertine, without breaking up the relation which he sustains to his mistresses. The directions given are such as would instantly change all sorts of masters into upright and righteous non-slaveholding masters. They directly and positively forbid all regarding, treating, and holding of human beings as property. They absolutely and forever cut off all trespass upon personal manhood rights. No man can give to his servant that which is "just," and regard him as property. Such regarding is gross injustice—injustice *per se*. No man can give to his servant that which is "just," and *treat* him as property. Such treating is gross injustice—injustice *per se*. No man can give to his servant that which is "just," and *hold* him as property. Such holding is gross injustice—injustice *per se*. The moment the slaveholder gives to his slaveservant that which is "just," he ceases to regard, or treat, or hold him as property. The moment he does that, he ceases to be a slaveholder, and his slaveservant drops the *slave*, and becomes a servant. No man can give to his servant that which is "equal," and *regard* him as property. All such regarding is great degradation—partial and unequal. No man can give to his servant that which is "equal," and *treat* him as property. All such treating is great degradation—partial and unequal. No man can give to his servant that which is "equal," and *hold* him as property. All such holding is great degradation—partial and unequal. And there is not a slave-owner on all the face of the earth who would not so judge, if the tables were turned, and the chattel principle should fasten its base grip upon himself. It is utterly impossible to apply these directions to the relation of slave-servants and slave-masters without abolishing the relation of slave and owner. As, therefore, these directions evidently contemplate the continuance of the relation involved in the terms master and servant, that relation could not have been that of slave and owner: for the moment they touch that relation they annihilate it.

The moral legislation in these two passages is very remarkable—remarkable for its brevity, breadth, and completeness. It is applicable to all masters, and covers the whole ground of mastership. It recognizes human equality fully; and, by one single enactment, imposes the great law of love upon all masters on the face of the earth. It instantly transmutes all masters, whether in English factories, on Yankee farms, on board pirate vessels, in the general's tent, in banditti dens, on slave plantations, in Turkish seraglios, or anywhere else on God's earth, into upright, righteous, non-slaveholding, and non-oppressing masters, regarding, treating, and holding their servants as equal *men*, and sacredly regarding all their rights as such. It is legislation that is perfect, final, and universal. It really embraces all that needs to be said to all sorts of masters. It gives them full liberty to exist, but puts them all alike under the great law of equal manhood, equal brotherhood, equal creatureship before God. This law instantly abolishes all chattelhood, all trespass upon personal manhood rights, all oppression, all injustice, all partial and unequal respect of persons. Such is the breadth and completeness of New Testament legislation for masters. In its atmosphere no slave-owner can draw a single breath.

CHAPTER XVIII.

OF THE DUTIES OF SERVANTS.

SEC. 1.—1 *Cor.* vii: 20–24.

IN examining those passages which refer to the duties of servants, the question before us is, Whether there is any thing in them which so modifies the word *servant* as necessarily to restrict its signification to the sense of *slave?* The question in regard to each passage is, "Is it so modified as to make it clearly and unequivocally refer specifically to *slaves?*" It must be so modified, else such sense can not be admitted.

We will examine and comment upon these passages in their order.

1 Cor. vii: 20–24—"Let every man abide in the same calling wherein he was called. Art thou called being a servant? Care not for it: but if thou mayest be made free, use it rather. For he that is called in the Lord, being a servant, is the Lord's freeman: likewise, also, he that is called, being free, is Christ's servant. Ye are bought with a price; be not ye the servants of men. Brethren, let every man, wherein he is called, therein abide with God."

In this passage the Apostle lays down the "general rule that converts should not quit that state of life wherein they were at conversion." To illustrate the rule, he adduces the case of *servants*. Now, in this whole passage, there is neither word, phrase, nor circumstance that in any way modifies the term δοῦλος, *doulos*, "*servants*," so as in the least to limit or restrict its meaning. It is used throughout in its unmodified, general sense. "Art thou called, being a servant?" Any sort of servant. As far as the simple inquiry before us is concerned, nothing more is necessary to be said. To multiply words is labor simply to prove a negative, when there is nothing to establish the affirmative. But in regard to the general sense of this passage, one or two things need to be remembered.

1. It should be particularly noticed, that the direction given in this passage is a *general* and not a *universal* rule. In the nature of the case, it can not be universal. (1.) It must be limited by the nature of the condition or calling in which the convert to Christianity found himself. That condition, or calling, must be a right and righteous calling, else the direction itself is incorrect and improper. "Let every man abide in the same calling wherein he was called," with the implied limitation that the *calling itself* is right and proper. The calling of the servant is such; and although it is better, on many accounts, to be a free man than to be a servant, yet, if needful, there is nothing degrading or improper in being a servant. Servitude is a necessity of human society; and if a man will throw aside the

16

feeling of slavish inferiority, and assert his own proper manhood as the creature of God and honored servant of Christ, it matters but little if his calling be that of a servant.   But the calling of the Thugs in India, who pretend to have a special, divine appointment to strangle, murder, and rob their fellow-beings for a livelihood, is an unrighteous and iniquitous calling: and this rule can not apply to that.   It can not apply to any unrighteous and iniquitous calling whatever.   As a *general rule*, it is good for a man to abide in the calling wherein he is called, provided always that calling is right and righteous.   (2.) This rule must have another limitation.   It is good for a man to abide by this rule, if he has chosen the calling to which he is *adapted*. No man in his senses supposes that Dr. Milnor or President Finney violated this rule, and sinned against God, in abandoning the calling of the law for that of the Gospel ministry.   If a man mistakes his calling at first, this rule surely allows him to correct his mistake.

There may be other exceptions to this rule.   In the nature of things the rule is a general one, subject to several limitations.   It will not do, therefore, to insist that, according to this apostolic direction, the slave must remain a slave, because that is his calling.   On the contrary, we insist that this rule has no application whatever to slaves, as rendering slave service.   Unchattelized servitude is a righteous and needful calling.   Slave servitude is an unrighteous, unneedful, and iniquitous calling.   The calling of a servant is right and proper, and no degradation, though compassed about with some disadvantages. The calling of a slave is abnormal and unfit—an evil to be escaped from. And this rule of the Apostle has no more application to slaves than it has to the imprisoned victims of piracy on the high seas. What if the pirate chief should very piously begin to preach from the Bible to his captured victims the propriety of their quietly "abiding in their calling" as prisoners? How ridiculous, absurd, and impious! But not a whit more ridiculous and impious than is the pious whining of slaveholders about their slaves abiding quietly in the same calling wherein they were called. How came the slave to be in the degrading and iniquitous calling of a slave? Precisely as the victims of the pirate crew on the high seas are in the calling of prisoners on board the pirate vessel: *by force and robbery!* Every slave is the victim of gross robbery, and a practical compulsion which he can not resist; and it would be just as fit and agreeable to right reason and the moral sense for the pirate chief to apply this Bible rule about keeping to one's calling, to his prisoners, and tell them that that was their *"calling,"* and that they ought to be faithful and obedient in it, as it is for pro-slavery people to seek to daub over the slaves with this same Apostolic mortar, to whom it was never tempered, and for whom it was never designed. Chattelhood is not a *calling:* it is only a stupendous wrong, affixed by human selfishness to the righteous calling of the servant. The slaveholder has no right to "abide" at all in perpetrating it: and the slave is under no obligation to abide in subjection to it. It is a good rule that all people, even servants of all classes, should keep to their respective callings, provided they are right and righteous, and they are adapted to them. This is common sense. But to stretch the rule beyond this is simple perversion. Neither Indian Thugs, nor pirates, nor gamblers, nor slaveholders, nor men-stealers, nor rum-sellers, can find any shelter under this good and wholesome Apostolic injunction. None of these things pertain to the servitude of which the Apostle is speaking in this passage under consideration. They are no part nor portion of it. They do not belong to it. They constitute no element of it. They are simply illegal and contraband super-additions, to which the injunctions of this passage have no application.

2. "But if thou mayest be made free, use it rather." It is better, on many accounts, to have the full reponsibilities of a free citizen and manager of one's own affairs, free from all dictation and control from others, than to occupy the inferior station of a servant. There are many advantages in being an independent citizen, at the head of one's own affairs, over any position of service for others. This, too, is common sense. It is safe, encouraging, and elevating advice for all unchattelized servants engaged in a right and righteous servitude, of whatever sort. The spirit of this advice inspires the heart of the

field laborer, the factory operative, the apprentice in the shop, *the servant* everywhere. It is good advice for him to hear, to receive, and to follow: good for himself, good for his employer, and good for the public. It is perfectly adapted to his relations: in perfect harmony with them. But who does not see that this is advice totally unadapted to the relations of chattel slaves? What mean the Southern police and slave-catching blood-hounds, our fugitive slave laws, and all this hue and cry about enticing slaves away from their owners, if the apostolic advice, divinely given, is, that slaves should seek to gain their freedom? Who does not know that such advice as this is totally impracticable, and not to be tolerated, for a single moment, in any slave-holding community? and that it would produce endless collision and warfare between slaves and their owners? Given the relation of slave and owner, and establish that, and this apostolic advice is totally inadmissible.

3. There is other bad advice in this passage to be given to slaves. It is that "the higher law" is to be their undeviating rule of action. "For he that is called in the Lord, being a servant, is the Lord's freeman: likewise also he that is called being free, is Christ's servant. Ye are bought with a price; be not ye the servants of men." Every servant, then, is bought with a price away from all service to men, to be supremely the servant of Christ. This is in direct conflict with the authority which every slaveholder must assume and exercise over his

chattel slave. It is in direct conflict with the authority which the pirate chief must exercise over his imprisoned captives. It is advice which exalts obedience to Christ above every thing else, and makes every other service subservient to that. It is advice which can be given with safety and propriety only to men and women unchattelized. For them, though servants, it is good, and wholesome, and safe.

4. "Ye are bought with a price." To understand this as a figurative allusion to the slave traffic, in which, with infinite degradation and wrong, human beings are bought and sold as chattel property like the dumb brutes, and, as thus illustrating the relation which Christ sustains to his people, as many do, is certainly monstrous enough. To make Christ call himself the *slaveholder* of his people, and to make him call them his *slaves*, is surely a great outrage upon Christian common sense. Some commentators, who have done this in one or two instances, have not had courage to carry the shocking indecency straight through the Bible, as consistency demanded. It sounds a little too bad for the most stolid Bible interpreter to make the "voice that came out" of "the great white throne" say, "Praise our God, all ye his *slaves;*" (Rev. xix: 5;) and to surround that throne with *slaves*, with Moses and the prophets among the number! Such ideas of the relations of God to his people, and of Him to them, are manifestly too grossly unfit to bear much repetition.

The beauty of this figurative language, which Paul uses more than once, " Ye are bought with a price," can be fully understood only by referring to the ancient idea of servitude. Anciently, and always among the Jews, the servants were unchattelized servants; and yet they were called "bought with money." This phrase, "bought with money," describes a common transaction in the Hebrew family, and connected with the economy of the Hebrew household; namely, that by which individuals, without infringing in the least upon their true and proper manhood, were attached to the Hebrew household, by buying. Money was paid: on this condition the individual united himself voluntarily to the household, to be under its government and control, and to do service therefor. This service was voluntary, cordial, and manly. The arrangement was mutual, and had in it all the sacredness of a family relationship. So, a great price has been paid to attach all penitent and believing souls to the great family of redeemed ones on earth and in heaven. Christ himself has volunteered the price, the sublimest gratuity which the universe ever beheld. Bought with this price, believers voluntarily enter into relationship with the great family of the holy, and with Jesus, the eternal head thereof. This is a relationship and an attachment vastly higher and more sacred than any thing merely earthly. It really absorbs all other relationships. It is mutual and close—infinitely removed from all idea of slavery. Christ has paid the price: on this basis the

penitent soul unites himself, by faith, to Christ and
his great family, to be under his control, and to
render to him a service, voluntary, supreme, affection-
ate, and hearty. When thus introduced into this
higher and diviner family relationship, he ceases, in
a very important sense, to be the servant of men.
" Be not ye the servants of men."

Sec. 2.—*Eph.* vi: 5-8.

"Servants, be obedient to them that are *your*
masters according to the flesh, with fear and trem-
bling, in singleness of your heart, as unto Christ:
Not with eye-service, as men-pleasers; but as the
servants of Christ, doing the will of God from the
heart; With good will doing service, as to the Lord,
and not to men: Knowing that whatsoever good
thing any man doeth, the same shall he receive of
the Lord, whether he be bond or free."

It will be noticed that the word "*your*," in this
first verse, is printed in italics in our translation,
indicating that the word is not found in the original
Greek. If we leave the word "*your*" out entirely,
and read the verse as it stands in the Greek, we shall
get nearer the true sense. "Servants, be obedient
to the masters according to the flesh." The word
δοῦλος, *doulos,* "*servant*," (or rather, δοῦλοι, *douloi,*
"*servants*,") is used in these verses in its naked,
unmodified form: and being thus unmodified, it has
its general sense. It means "*servants*." To give it

the limited, specific sense of *slaves*, is a violation of all grammatical and rhetorical rules. The word which is translated "*masters*," is precisely the same in the original Greek as in the passage which we have already examined in the Epistle to the Colossians, and has the same sense here as there. Both terms are unmodified, and are, therefore, used in a general sense. Consequently, there is not, in this passage, the remotest allusion to slaves and slave-owners, any more than there is to pirates and pirate-victims, or to Roman inquisitors and their victims. The passage pertains to *servants* and *masters*, and not to any of these other things.

In regard to the particular directions contained in this passage, and its general scope, we offer the following remarks:

1. It is very manifest that the *relation of servant and master* is assumed and acknowledged in this passage as a right and proper relation. Now, the relation of *slave and owner* is intrinsically wrong, improper, and unlawful. It is unrighteous trespass upon inalienable manhood rights. To assume or acknowledge that this relation is right and proper, is gross falsehood. It never is and never can be right and proper. It is universally and always unlawful trespass. Of necessity, therefore, the relation assumed and referred to in this passage under the terms "*servants* and *masters*," can not be the relation of *slaves* and *owners*. It must be something else. To admit that the relation assumed in this passage is that of *slaves* and *owners*, would con-

17

vict the Apostle of gross blindness and gross falsehood. By no possibility, therefore, can this passage
refer to *slaves* and *owners*.

2. The directions in this passage of Scripture are
necessary, common-sense directions, addressed to all
servants. It is right and proper for all servants in
the full possession of all their manhood rights, to be
obedient to masters according to the flesh. Indeed,
it is impossible to be servants without rendering
such obedience. Obedience, subjection—is necessarily included in the relation. As long as servants
sustain the relation of servants, they are bound to
obey their masters or employers. It belongs to the
master to direct, and to them to obey. This is common sense, and needs everywhere to be understood
and remembered. It is exactly the right sort of
advice to be given to servants—good for the servant,
good for the master.

3. This, however, must be a *general direction*, and,
of course, subject to some limitations. Obedience
must be limited *by the nature of the* requisitions *of
the master*. If these requisitions are unrighteous
and wicked, so that obedience involves moral wrong,
this command does not apply. Servants are not to
disobey God, in order to obey masters. They are
under no obligation to obey unrighteous commands,
obedience to which would be criminal. If the master commands murder, or licentious pollution, or any
other intrinsic wrong, his command imposes no obligation upon the servant. If Aquila had commanded
Paul, when he served Aquila at his house in Corinth,

in the tent-making business, to take his youngest child and cast it into the Saronic Gulf to perish in its waters, such command would have imposed no obligation upon the serving Paul to obey it. Paul, no doubt, whenever he found it necessary to "work out," as he did under the direction of Aquila and Priscilla, was a good and obedient servant, but he loved the higher law.

Neither does the command in this passage apply to *enforced*, *unrighteous*, and degrading servitude, such as slave servitude. It may be *expedient* to render some sort of obedience, to some extent, in such cases, but such obedience is not due to any claim which the oppressing master possesses in the case. It is not due to any obligation which this command imposes, for it does not apply in the case. It may have been highly expedient, that is, due to himself and due to the universe, for Dr. Livingstone to lie very quiet and obedient under the yawning nose of the African lion, which, by a hearty shake of the great explorer, had effectually taught him on which side the power lay; but he was under no obligation to his African majesty to render such obedience, though he was, for the time being, his master. The captives of a Bedouin marauding party may find it very expedient to obey their murderous masters, but this command which we are considering imposes no obligation to such obedience. And why? Simply because the servitude is an enforced, un-righteous, and oppressive servitude. It may be very expedient for the chattelized and degraded slave to obey his owner, who, as oppressor, is his master for the time being; but this command does not apply to his case. And the reason is, that the kind of servitude is an enforced, unrighteous, and oppressive one. This command assumes and recognizes the relation of master and servant, placing both on an equal footing as to individual manhood and its rights, making obedience the duty of the servant, and direction and control the duty of the master. To this relation the command applies. As to the relation of slave and owner, it says nothing: but in the nature of the case, to this relation it does not and can not apply.

4. This command of obedience on the part of servants, as well as all that pertains to the relation of servant and master, is expressly limited by the Apostle, by the great higher obligation to Christ, as the Supreme Lord and King. Servants are to be, first of all and supremely, servants of Christ: and all their service to men is to be subservient to this their higher service to Christ. This is the principal thing in these instructions to servants in this passage under consideration. Now, this great and fundamental limitation is perfectly consistent and harmonious with the righteous relation of master and servant; but totally inconsistent with the relation of owner and slave. " Not with eye-service as men-pleasers; but as the servants of Christ, doing the will of God from the heart; With good-will doing service, as to the Lord, and not to men." Obedience on the principle of the great law of benevolence or good-will, and

wholly subservient to that; and the whole responsibility of rendering such higher-law obedience thrown
wholly upon the servant. And then, in the ninth
verse, the masters are commanded to act on the same
principle toward their servants, and, in conclusion,
they are told that with God "there is no respect of
persons," plainly implying that there should not be
with men. So both master and servant are put upon a
level; the servant to obey directions, in subserviency
to the law of obedience to Christ, and the master to
exercise control, in subserviency to the same law.
All this is perfectly consistent with the relation of
servant and master, but totally inconsistent with the
relation of slave and owner. Slavery universally
practically abrogates the higher law for all its slaves.
Preaching, in the true spirit of this passage of Scripture would not, for a moment, be tolerated on any
Southern plantation. It takes the servant and exalts him to his true position and dignity as a man, a
creature, and child of God, whose conscience, whose
moral agency, whose true freedom and personal responsibility are to be under no authority, no control,
no direction below that of the Lord Jehovah, whose
he is, and for whose glory he was made. This is good
and wholesome preaching for servants and masters,
but perfectly suicidal and fatal for slaves and owners. The two can not possibly be put together.
They never are put together. The only possible
way in which this command can be made to apply
to slaves and their owners is, by abolishing the
slavery and exalting the slave to the condition of·

an unchattelized servant, and subtracting from the
owner his robber-ownership and making him simply
a master. This would be changing the relation of
slave and owner to that of servant and master: and
then the command would apply. But this command
has not the least possible or conceivable application
whatever to slaves or slaveholders as such. That is
not the relation which it contemplates. Of that
relation it says nothing.

Sec. 3.—*Col.* iii: 22–25; iv: 1.

This passage is very similar to the one in Ephesians which we have just examined. We will quote
it, however, entire, with the first verse of the next
chapter, which manifestly belongs to it. "Servants,
obey in all things *your* masters according to the
flesh; not with eye-service, as men-pleasers; but in
singleness of heart, fearing God: And whatsoever
ye do, do it heartily, as to the Lord, and not unto
men; Knowing that of the Lord ye shall receive
the reward of the inheritance: for ye serve the Lord
Christ. But he that doeth wrong, shall receive for
the wrong which he hath done: and there is no respect of persons." Col. iv: 1—"Masters, give unto
your servants that which is just and equal; Knowing that ye also have a Master in heaven."

Here, the word "*servants*," δοῦλοι, *douloi*, is used
in its simple, unqualified form, and hence in its general sense. This is New Testament usage. Hence,
this passage can not relate specifically to slaves and

their owners. It relates to servants and masters. The "*your*" in the first verse is a superfluity of the translators. "Servants, obey in all things the masters according to the flesh."

As already intimated, this passage is very similar to the passage already examined in Ephesians. The writer is the same, and the scope of the passage and the directions in it are much the same. The persons spoken of are "*servants*" and "*masters:*" the relation is that of servitude—that of servant and master. This does not include the relation of slave and owner, and has nothing to do with it. The passage is subject to the same limitations as that in Ephesians by the same writer. Like that, it is expressly guarded by the all-pervading presence of the higher law. Servants are to be under that law in all their service to masters. Masters are to be under the same law, and to give to the servants "that which is just and equal." All this is in perfect harmony with the righteous relation of servant and master: but perfectly impossible when applied to a state of slavery. The moment it is thus applied, it either totally abolishes the slavery, and transmutes it into righteous servitude, or creates a deadly and fatal antagonism.

In regard to these three passages of Apostolic writing, found in these three epistles to churches, we especially beg of the reader to notice this one thing. While the propriety of obedience on the part of the servants is admitted, and the duty of obedience is enjoined, the main drift of each of these passages aims distinctly to *exalt the servant*, and make a God's man of him, precisely on a level, as to his manhood and its rights, with the master. If the reader will carefully examine each of these passages, he will see, at once, that this statement is literally true. It is not the object of these passages at all to thrust the servant down into a dog's place, and degrade the man out of him, but to take him away from all this, and put him on a level with the master, an equal creature and child of God. The *obedience* is not dwelt upon—but the *exaltation* of that obedience. The obedience is admitted as right and proper, but in all these passages the greatest care is taken that it shall not degrade the servant; that it shall not trespass upon one single right of his as God's man, God's creature, God's free, moral agent, God's child. Not one of these passages can be applied to chattel slavery without instantly consuming it.

CHAPTER XIX.

1 TIM. VI: 1, 2; TITUS, II: 9, 10.

THE directions to obedience of servants to masters, in the three passages which we have examined from the church Epistles of Paul, are couched in the simplest and most general form. "Let the servants be obedient to the masters." Or, perhaps more accurately, "Let the servants pay good attention to what the masters direct." In the personal Epistles of Paul we meet with two other passages which contain directions to servants, in which the language used is somewhat different, and somewhat more particular. These passages are found, one in the First Epistle to Timothy, and the other in the Epistle to Titus. It will be convenient to quote and examine these two passages together.

1 Tim. vi: 1, 2—"Let as many servants as are under the yoke count their own masters worthy of all honor, that the name of God and his doctrine be not blasphemed. And they that have believing masters, let them not despise them, because they are brethren; but rather do them service, because they are faithful and beloved, partakers of the benefit." Titus, ii: 9, 10—"*Exhort* servants to be obedient unto their own masters, and to please them

well in all things; not answering again; not purloining, but showing all good fidelity; that they may adorn the doctrine of God our Savior in all things."

In both of these passages servants are spoken of with special reference to "*their own* masters." In both of these passages, also, the word which is translated "*masters*" is different, in the original Greek, from that which Paul uses in the other epistles to designate masters. It is a word of frequent occurrence in classic Greek, but does not often occur in the New Testament; not more than ten times. Paul uses it only once (2 Tim. ii; 22) except in these two passages before us: and in that one instance it manifestly refers to Christ. Peter uses it once, in speaking of servants and masters. In all the other places where it is used in the New Testament, it refers to God or Christ. The proper meaning of this word, δεσπότης, *despotees*, is, "*the head of a family, pater familias.*"* The head of a family is, in an important sense, the "master" of the household. He is the man to whom servants should be subject. There is not, therefore, in the word "*masters*," which is used in these passages, the remotest allusion to slavery or slave-owners. We have, however, in the peculiar phraseology of these passages, a distinct allusion to the Jewish idea of servitude, and of the household. The servants are spoken of as being attached to particular households, and as

* Dr. Robinson.

having the head of the family for their master.
Such allusion would have been less appropriate in
epistles addressed to Gentile churches, but it is very
significant when found in epistles directed to Christian bishops familiar with the Jewish Scriptures.

Connected with the word δοῦλοι, *douloi,* "*servants,*" in the first verse of the passage in the Epistle
to Timothy, we have the qualifying phrase, "under
the yoke." "Servants under the yoke." Does this
phrase mean *slaves?* Is this the idiomatic form of
expression which the sacred writers use to designate
slaves? If it is, then we have, at last, found the
specific and peculiar form of speech which, in the
New Testament, denotes a *slave,* and we shall know
exactly where to look for the slaves, and where to
look for servants, and henceforward all will be plain.
But it so happens that this form of speech is used
in the New Testament only in this one solitary
place. If this is Paul's peculiar and idiomatic form
of speech for *slave,* the presumption is, that when
he means slave, he uses this same form of speech.
This presumption becomes a certainty when we
have found, as is the case, that he uses no other
form of speech for this purpose. This would settle it, that he means *slave* in no other place in his
writings.

But there is no evidence that this peculiar form
of speech does mean slave, as used in Paul's writings. He uses the word "*yoke*" in only one other
place, namely, Gal. v: 1, in which passage he calls
the obedience of the man who seeks to keep the law

without faith in Christ "A yoke of bondage." This yoke of bondage was not chattel slavery. In Phil. iv: 3, he uses the same word coupled with the pre-position *with*, (σύν, *sŭn*,) "I entreat thee also, true *yoke-fellow*," etc. He here calls his brother Christ-ian a "*yoke-fellow*," alluding, perhaps, to that beau-tiful saying of our Savior, recorded in Matt. xi: 29, 30: "Take my yoke upon you, and learn of me; . . . . . For my yoke is easy and my burden is light:" in which words Christ recommends his "*yoke*" for the relief of those who "labor and are heavy laden." But this evidently is not the yoke of chattel slavery, and has no allusion to it. Peter makes use of this same word in his speech in the council at Jerusalem on the subject of circumcision, Acts xv: 10. This word also occurs in Rev. vi: 5: "And I beheld, and lo, a black horse; and he that sat on him had *a pair of balances* in his hand." In Matt. xix: 6, and Mark x: 9, a verb is used derived from the same root, which refers to the joining together of husband and wife. In Luke ii: 24, "A *pair* of turtle doves," and xiv: 19, "I have bought five yoke of oxen," we have another form of the same word, in which the primary meaning of the word appears. These examples embrace the whole of the New Testament usage. We have, then, the yoke of the Mosaic law, the yoke of Christ, the yoke of marriage, five yoke of oxen, one yoke of turtle doves, the yoke that was in the man's hand that rode upon the black horse, and the yoke of servi-tude referred to by Paul in this passage to Timothy.

From all this usage it is manifest that this word "*yoke*" has no particular and special reference to chattel slavery. So wide is its figurative use that it is properly applied to the service of Christ, which Paul takes a great deal of pains to show is the highest kind of freedom, and not bondage. From this usage it is manifest that any sort of allegiance might be called a *yoke*. The yoke of common servitude might be more or less severe, according to circumstances. In some households, where the engagement was for life, or for a long period, it might be very severe.

In our judgment, Paul uses the word δοῦλος, *doulos*, "*servant*," in this passage in its general sense, as he does in other places, adding the phrase "under the yoke," to indicate simply the state of allegiance or servitude in which the servants were held: that he acknowledges the propriety and lawfulness of the relation of master and servant just as he does elsewhere, and with the same limitations: and that both of these passages do not differ in scope and spirit from the passages already examined in his other epistles. Like them, they are addressed to servants independent of their masters: like them, they contemplate servants as true men having all the rights of proper manhood: like them, they enjoin subjection and obedience to the master: like them, they put the servant under the authority of the higher law of obedience to God: and like them, they refer to the relation of servant and master, but contain no allusion to the relation of slave and owner.

CHAPTER XX.

INFERENCES AND REMARKS SUGGESTED BY FORE-GOING EXPOSITIONS.

IN regard to these several passages of Scripture which we have been examining from the writings of Paul, we wish to remark here, that there are two or three considerations in reference to them, taken as a whole, and as containing the instructions of the New Testament addressed particularly to servants, to which special attention is invited.

1. All these passages manifestly refer to the same subject, and contain substantially the same instructions and directions. These passages all plainly relate to one and the same thing: and the directions in them are precisely similar.

2. Now, if Paul meant *slaves* in these passages, it is very singular that he did not say *slaves*. He was not afraid to say "*men-stealers*" when he meant that. He uses the word δοῦλος, *doulos*, in connections and relations where the sense can not possibly be *slave*. His general usage of the word is clearly in the sense of *servant*, and not in the sense of *slave*. In the first line even in his Epistle to the Romans, his first Epistle in order in the New Testament, he uses it in this sense: "Paul, a servant of Jesus Christ." Now, it is very singular that he should

use this same word, without qualification, in the different and specific sense of *slave, whenever he gives directions to servants, and nowhere else.* This is very strange indeed. But if these passages refer specifically to slaves, this is precisely what he has done. This would convict him of the most wonderful literary freak that ever was perpetrated, at least by an inspired writer. For it was just as easy for him to say slaves in language that meant *slaves,* as it was for him to say slaves in language that meant *servants.*

3. If Paul, in all these passages, does use the word δοῦλος, *doulos,* in the limited, specific sense of *slave,* as most of the commentators interpret and expound, and if Peter, also, in his one single direction to servants, means *slaves,* as many understand, then we have not one solitary direction or exhortation to any other class or classes of servants, as such, in the entire New Testament. Paul, the great Apostle and chief writer of the New Testament, gives repeated directions to *slaves,* but not one direction whatever to *servants* of any sort: for a slave is not necessarily a servant, any more than a horse-jockey's horses are all actually employed in service. Paul, guided by the unerring wisdom of inspiration, singles out *slaves,* and commands and exhorts them, but has not one word of instruction, command, or exhortation, in all his writings, for any or all of the multiplied and various classes of unchattelized servants to be found in all the world, or in any age. This is very singular indeed. It is strange, indeed,

that the pen of inspiration, writing for the instruction of the world in all coming time, should be very
particular to tell slaves to obey their owners—a
direction against which, in its unqualified sense,
human reason utterly rebels, as much as it would
against the command to pirate captives to obey their
pirate masters—but should entirely overlook all
other servants and classes of servants. Husbands
and wives; parents and children; rulers and subjects; brethren and brethren; teachers and taught;
elder and younger; and, at last, but quite prominent,
according to this interpretation, *slaves* and *owners*,
are all commanded and exhorted; but servants and
masters of all sorts and classes are skipped over in
profound silence. Those that can believe this, must
find reasons for their belief as best they can. We
believe no such thing. We believe most fully that
masters and servants, and not *slaves and owners*, are
the subjects of discourse and of command in all these
passages which we have been examining.

4. The absurdity of making δοῦλος, *doulos*, mean
slave, may be illustrated. The word *"bread"* is frequently used in the Bible. Like δοῦλος, *doulos*, it
is a general term, and is so used as to imply sanction of the use of bread as an article of food. But
"bread may either be made of the flour of wheat,
of rye, of barley, of corn, of oats; or it may be
made of the starch of the potato, or of various other
farinaceous vegetables; it may be made even of
bran, even of spurred rye, than which few poisons
are more destructive to health, or fatal to the life

of man. Moreover, the same may be fermented or unfermented—debased by the mixture of innutritious ingredients, and even of the most deadly poisons; but *however made*, or *of whatever* made, *it is still called bread.* But because it is so called, are we to believe, when bread is spoken of in terms" which imply commendation and sanction of its use, "that among all the kinds of bread which exist, the very vilest of them is had in contemplation" and especially and specifically meant? "Or because the use of bread," as the word is employed in the Bible, is impliedly or expressly "sanctioned in the Bible, sanctioned habitually, sanctioned even at the communion-table, are we to believe that" "that sort of bread which is known to be destructive of health and even of life"* is the particular kind of bread which is specifically and expressly meant and sanctioned? Such conclusion would be preposterous, absurd, and ridiculous. But this case is precisely analagous to the use of δοῦλος, *doulos, servant*, in the New Testament. *"Bread"* is a general term: δοῦλος, *doulos, servant*, is a general term: 'it is no more absurd to single out the vilest and most poisonous kind of bread, and affirm that that was the bread which was used and sanctioned at the communion-table when Christ himself presided in person, than it is to single out the vilest and most villainous kind of servitude that Heaven's rolling sun ever shone upon, as Conybeare and Howson, and a multitude of other commentators of less learn-

* Pres. Nott, D. D.

18

·ing and note have actually done, and affirm that that was the particular kind of servitude meant in all the passages where Paul speaks of the duties of servants and masters. Such a procedure is totally unwarranted, preposterous, and absurd.

5. This view which we have taken of the sense and usage of *δοῦλος, doulos, servant,* in the Pauline writings, is confirmed by direct, incidental testimony from his own pen. Very fortunately he has given us, quite clearly, in his Epistle to the Galatians, his idea of a servant. It corresponds exactly with the Abrahamic and Jewish idea of a servant. In Gal iv: 1, it is written: "Now I say, That the heir, as long as he is a child, differeth nothing from a servant, though he be lord of all." No man in his senses would ever make such a comparison as this, if *servant* meant *slave.* No slaveholder ever thought of making such a statement as this, as to the equality of his slaves with his children. The subjection of the child and heir in the household never is like that of the slave. It "differeth" from it totally. But it is very like that of the free, unchattelized servant in the Hebrew household, patterned after the old Abrahamic type, with its "justice and judgment." This was Paul's idea of servant. This is the idea that we are to attach to the word *servant* when it occurs in his writings.

CHAPTER XXI.

EXPOSITION OF 1 PETER, II: 18.

THERE is one other passage, which is found in the First Epistle of Peter, which speaks of the duties of servants. This is sometimes quoted as belonging to the same class with the passages which we have examined in the writings of Paul. On account of its different phraseology in the original Greek, some writers have given it a different signification and application. Some quote it as referring to slavery, others reject it as having nothing to do with slavery.

We will endeavor to present, in few words, what we understand to be its true meaning and bearing upon the subject before us.

The passage is as follows: "Servants, *be* subject to *your* masters with all fear; not only to the good and gentle, but also to the froward."

1. In regard to this passage, it may be remarked, in the first place, that the *form* of the passage is general. The pronoun "*your*" is not in the original text. The sense may be expressed in this way: "Let the servants be subject to the masters."

2. In the second place, it is to be noticed, that this direction is found in immediate connection with other general directions touching the relations of life. Before it we have, in the thirteenth verse and

onward, directions in regard to the duty of obeying
civil magistrates. Following it, in the next chapter,
wives and husbands are addressed. The passage
which we are examining is the only passage in this
epistle which refers to the duties of servants. It is
nàtural, therefore, to suppose that Peter, in this
passage, is speaking of servants in the general sense:
and it is very unnatural to suppose that, while the
whole epistle is remarkable for its universality, he
has, in this passage, singled out a particular kind of
servants, and laid injunctions upon them, and left
all other servants entirely out of the account. He
speaks of civil rulers and subjects, and gives general directions—directions applicable to all rulers
and subjects. He speaks of wives and husbands,
and gives directions in the same way. It would
seem almost morally certain that, in speaking of
servants and masters, he would use these terms in
the same general sense. We certainly think he has
done this.

3. But the terms used by Peter, in this passage,
are different from those used by Paul in speaking
of servants and masters, and are such as can not,
with any propriety, be referred to slaves and
owners. The word, in the original Greek, which is
translated "*servants*" is not δοῦλοι, *douloi*, which is
the word Paul uses, but another word, (οἰκέται, *oike-
tai*,) whose proper meaning is *one living in the same
house*, or *house-companion*.* The word for "*masters*"
is the same as in Titus, ii: 9, and, as there, denotes

* Dr. Robinson.

*the head of a family, pater familias.** This corresponds exactly with the Hebrew idea of servant and
master: servant, an attaché of the household; master, the family head, or chief.   Peter, being thoroughly a Jew, and having less acquaintance with
Gentiles and Gentile literature than Paul, would be
very likely to use the word οἰκέτης, *oiketees, house-
companion,* instead of δοῦλος, *doulos,* to mean
servant.   This is the true Abrahamic-Hebrew idea
of servant.   This was Peter's idea of servant, and
hence he has selected words and language in the
Greek that very nicely and beautifully express, not
the Roman or Grecian idea of servant, but the pure,
native Jewish idea with which he was familiar, and
to which he had always been accustomed.   Failing
to notice or recognize this important fact, many
writers have been much puzzled to understand
exactly what Peter meant in this passage.   It is
very harsh and arbitrary, indeed, nay, utterly inadmissible, to apply this language to chattel slavery.
It is, also, very tame and narrow to refer this only
passage in Peter's epistle which speaks of the
duties of servants, to domestic, kitchen servants, as
some commentators have.   Neither of these interpretations is at all satisfactory.   In our judgment,
Peter uses the language he employs in this passage
in an enlarged, general sense.   The words are Greek,
the sense Hebrew.   *House-companion,* or, rather,
household-companion, is much the true Hebrew
idea of servant.   Peter, being altogether a Jew, and

---

* Dr. Robinson.

having had altogether a Hebrew education, would be very sure to select this identical language to designate servants in the general sense; while Paul, having more acquaintance with foreign customs and literature, and writing to and for foreigners, would be more likely to select δοῦλος, *doulos*, a term in the Greek more general, and one that would unequivocally cover the whole ground of servitude. The English translators, therefore, were entirely correct in retaining the word "*servant*," and in giving the passage a general signification, as they have, in our English Bible. The passage unquestionably refers to servitude in the general, righteous, Hebrew sense, and has not the remotest reference to chattel slavery. It relates to servants and masters, and contains no allusion whatever to slaves and owners.

CHAPTER XXII.

RECAPITULATION AND CONCLUSIONS.

1. IN this examination of the New Testament, we have seen that if the writers thereof had conformed simply to the proprieties of classic usage, their use of δοῦλος, *doulos*, which is the word they usually employ to denote *servant*, must have been as a general term. They would have used this word not in a specific, but in a general sense, corresponding with our English word *servant*.

2. We have also seen, that if they had followed Hebrew ideas, usages, and customs, as native Jews, they would surely have used δοῦλος, *doulos*, in a general sense, and not in the specific sense of *slave*.

3. We have further seen, from an extended and careful examination of various passages in which this word occurs, that their actual use of it is in the general sense—a sense corresponding with the sense of our word *servant* in English, and that it utterly forbids the specific sense of *slave*.

4. By a similar examination, we have seen that the writers of the New Testament never modify this term so as to give it the specific sense of slave. Or at least that it is not so modified in any of the passages that give directions to servants and masters.

Without such modification, such sense is entirely inadmissible.

5. There were other better terms at hand in the Greek language to use for *slave*, which they might have used, and which they were not afraid to use, as is manifest from 1 Tim. i: 10.

6. Furthermore, we have seen that the directions given in the passages where *servants* and *masters* are spoken of; are perfectly consonant with the general and righteous relation of master and servant, but utterly inconsistent with the different and narrower relation of slave and owner: that they elevate, sanctify, and make safe the former, while to the latter they are totally impracticable, or fatally destructive.

7. Hence, the conclusion is inevitable and irresistible, that the writers of the New Testament use the word δοῦλος, *doulos*, which is the only word used in the New Testament that is supposed to mean *slave*, universally in its general sense—a sense corresponding with the signification of our English word *servant*, and never in the specific sense of *slave*. The foregoing considerations, established beyond all contradiction, make this conclusion irrefragable. Our English translation is faithful and correct in this matter. Wherever the word *servant* occurs, the true meaning is *servant*, and not *slave*. So of the word *master :* wherever it occurs it means *master*, and not *slave-owner*.

Now, if Paul and the writers of the New Testament used these terms which we have been examining in a general sense, the *relation* which they had in mind in the use of these terms, must have been the relation of *servant* and *master*, and not the relation of slave and owner, pirate and captive, or any other such different and specific relation. This is self-evident.

1. It is also manifest that, since they used these terms very frequently, and without modification, and in numerous leading instances where any other sense is inadmissible, they always referred, in the use of these terms, to the *same relation*. There is nothing in their use of these terms to indicate that they did not use them in a uniform sense in this respect: namely, as always pointing to one and the same relation. The *relation*, therefore, of *servant and master*, and not the relation of slave and owner, is always the relation which is contemplated whenever these terms occur in the New Testament.

2. Hence, whenever *directions* are given to servants and masters, the *relation* assumed and recognized is not and can not be the relation of slave and owner, but that of servant and master. In all these directions this is the relation contemplated. There is no avoiding this conclusion, from the facts and demonstrations presented.

3. It is also this relation as a *right relation*. In all the passages in the New Testament which give directions to servants and masters, the relation implied in these terms is plainly assumed, and recognized, and treated, as a right and proper relation. It is in vain to deny this, as many anti-slavery men have done. The directions themselves manifestly

19

contemplate the continuance of the relation, and that it may be righteously sustained by both parties. But, since this relation is the righteous relation of servant and master, and not the unrighteous relation of slave and owner, its full recognition as righteous, by the inspired writers, is altogether proper. This recognition runs through the New Testament. The relation which is recognized in all those passages which give directions to servants and masters, is the relation of servant and master, and that as a right and proper relation.

4. But it must be that relation with all *needful limitations*, as we have already seen. The relation of servant and master has its limitations. These limitations are always assumed whenever the relation itself is referred to. The relation must be righteously sustained. All relations spoken of in the Bible have their limitations in the same way. The parental relation, for example, is a right one: it is everywhere assumed and recognized as such, in the Bible. It has its limitations, however. It must be righteously sustained. As the man hath not power in himself without the woman, it is right for the man to seek to become a father by the help of some one chosen woman. But the Bible would not sanction his seeking to become a father with every woman whom he might chance to meet. The propriety of the parental relation in itself would, by no means, give him that latitude. It has its righteous limitations. So has the righteous relation of servitude—the relation of servant and master. The

Bible recognizes its propriety, as it does all other right relations within the circle of these limitations: but never outside of them. This is assumed and implied in all the passages in the New Testament which give directions to servants and masters.

5. Hence there is not, in any of these passages, the remotest sanction, tolerance, or sufferance given either to slaveholding, or to the system of slavery, or to the relation of slave and owner. The relation spoken of is another relation entirely. It does not include the relation of slave and owner, and can never be stretched to embrace it. *It* is a separate matter entirely: a somewhat not implied or contemplated in these passages, and with which they have nothing to do. If, in addition to the relation of master and servant, servants should be forced to sustain the relation of breeding harlots to their masters, this would be a matter entirely distinct from, and not at all implied in, the relation of master and servant, and not falling under the same rules. Such servants would be obliged to get along with this extraneous oppression and wrong as best they might: but these commands, addressed to them as servants, would have no application to them as harlots. So of any other abuse. So of the relation of chattelhood. If the master should force the servant into the relation of slavery, in addition to that of servant, and make a chattel slave of him, this would be a new and extra relation not implied, or contemplated, or recognized at all in these directions to servants and masters. They refer to the relation

of servant and master, and have nothing to do with the other relation of slave and owner.

6. Hence again, since no such sanction, tolerance, or sufferance is elsewhere found in the New Testament, there is absolutely not the least shadow of sanction, toleration, or sufferance given to slavery, or to slaveholding, or to the relation of slave and owner, anywhere in the New Testament. Nothing nearer to this is sanctioned in the New Testament than unchattelized servitude, always guarded by righteous limitations. Of chattel slavery, the New Testament knows nothing, except as it learns from the Old Testament, that it is capital crime. The relation of *servant and master* is as frequently alluded to in the New Testament writings as any other relation; and it is uniformly so alluded to as to give it sanction as being right and proper. According to their teachings, this relation is rightly sustained when servants obey the directions of their masters, and when masters give unto their servants that which is just and equal. This makes the New Testament consistent with itself, and consistent with the great and eternal principles of rectitude and right which are laid down in the Word of God, and recognized in the human intelligence.

Does any one inquire, "What, then, are the particular teachings of the New Testament on the subject of slavery?" The answer is easy and brief. The Old Testament, from the beginning, had recognized the relation of master and servant as a right relation. It had, in the Mosaic code, legislated on this subject so as to protect and do justice to both master and servant. The relation of slave and owner it had set down, with terrible brevity, in the category of capital crimes. Ex. xxi: 16—"And he that stealeth a man, and selleth him, or if he be found in his hand, he shall surely be put to death." This, under the very shadow of Mount Sinai, while the earth still quaked greatly beneath the footsteps of the Almighty Jehovah. Deut. xxiv: 7—"If a man be found stealing any of his brethren of the children of Israel, and maketh merchandise of him, or selleth him; then that thief shall die; and thou shalt put evil away from among you." As capital "EVIL" it always treated it. This was sufficient. The New Testament finds the matter right there, and leaves it right there. The chattelizing of human beings is one of those gross crimes condemned by every precept and principle of God's law, and by every sentiment of right in the human reason, in regard to which nothing further, particular, and special needed to be said.

According to Paul, in his First Epistle to Timothy, i: 10, the Old Testament law on this subject was made for those who perpetrated the crime in all ages of the world. This was enough. Many forms of gross crime are passed over in silence by the writers of the New Testament, so far as any special or particular designation is concerned. Piracy, both as a system and as particular wickedness, is not so much as once named by them. Paul certainly could not have been ignorant of its wide-spread existence

in those times.   No special directions are given to
those who should become the victims of piratical
plunder or capture: and no special directions are
given in regard to the duties growing out of the
existence of piracy, or the relation of piracy.   Piracy
is as much a system as slavery is.   But the very
silence of the New Testament in regard to such
gross enormities, especially after the Old Testament
has spoken, and the voice of Jehovah from Mount
Sinai stands recorded there, is more terribly expres-
sive than any additional utterances could be.   This
silence proclaims to all the world that all God has
to say of chattel slavery is, that it is a capital
crime !   The very brevity of this legislation gives
it a fearful significance.   With this brief, direct,
unequivocal legislation, the Old Testament disposes
of this matter: the New Testament, fully endorsing
this legislation, in 1 Tim. i : 10, has nothing more
to add.   Without multiplying words, both Testaments promptly shake their garments of all com-
plicity with, and sanction of, chattel slavery.   Both
alike treat and condemn it as capital crime.

CHAPTER XXIII.

SPECIAL CHAPTER ON THE TWO RELATIONS (1) OF
SERVANT AND MASTER, AND (2) OF SLAVE AND
OWNER.

A LATE writer on the subject of slavery remarks,
that "The Mosaic statutes respecting the relation of
master and slave are obviously modifications and
amendments of a previously existing common law,
and are designed to ameliorate the condition of the
slave, to protect him from oppression, and to promote the gradual disuse and abolition of slavery." *
Other writers have seen very clearly that both the
Patriarchal history and the Mosaic code speak and
treat of servants and masters, and hence of servitude, as an existing state of things. This has been
already noticed in examining particular passages
of Scripture in the Mosaic writings. The Patriarchal history refers to, and speaks of, servitude,
servants and masters, as familiar matters, well
understood, and belonging to the settled arrangements of society. The Mosaic code proceeds to
legislate about servitude, servants and masters as
something already existing, and with which the

* L. Bacon: Slavery, p. 29.

people for whom that code was given were familiar. Of this there can be no doubt. The great mistake, however, of the quotation above, and with most writers on the subject of Bible servitude, lies in making the *relation* involved in these references to servitude, servants and masters, the relation of *slave and owner*, instead of the relation of *servant and master*. It has been already fully shown, we trust, in the progress of this work, that *the relation* implied in the allusions to servitude, servants and masters, in the Patriarchal history; *the relation* contemplated in the Mosaic legislation concerning servitude, servants and masters; and *the relation* recognized in the instructions given to servants and masters, in the New Testament, are one and the same relation; and that that relation is the relation of servant and master, and not the other relation of slave and owner. But we wish here to condense and sum up the argument, and present it in short space before the eye of the reader.

1. It is abundantly proved and admitted, that the words themselves that are translated *servant* and *master*, and the terms *bought* and *sold*, as used in the Mosaic writings, determine nothing as to the condition into which those were introduced who were thus bought and sold, and spoken of as servants. A candid and thorough examination demonstrates this, as Dr. Barnes, Dr. Cheever, and other learned men have fully shown. In Old Testament usage, these terms were entirely appropriate to free

men, freely applied to persons who could not have been chattel slaves. The words and terms used, therefore, decide nothing as to the relation of the persons to whom they are applied. These terms are just as applicable to free servants as to slave servants.

2. In the Patriarchal history, and in the Mosaic code, the master is never called *owner*, and the servant is never described as *property* beyond his services. This can be accounted for only on the supposition that the relation contemplated was the relation of master and servant, and not the relation of slave and owner. If this latter had been the relation contemplated, it would certainly have been specifically designated.

3. The condition into which servants were introduced, and the manner in which they were held and treated, have all the marks and characteristics which belong to a condition of free, unchattelized servitude, and none of the characteristics which belong to the peculiar condition of chattel slaves. This fact, which is incontrovertible, really settles the whole question. For the real question is not *how* servants in the Patriarchal households, and under the Mosaic code, came to be servants there; but how they were held when there: as free servants, or as slave servants? Now, it is incontestible that Abraham's treatment of his servants was utterly inconsistent with a state of slavery, and consistent only with a state of freedom: and that

the regulations of the Mosaic code are totally inconsistent with a state of slavery, and consistent only
with a state of freedom.   The relation implied,
therefore, in both cases, must have been the relation
of servant and master, and not the relation of slave
and owner.

4. The concomitants of slavery are totally wanting in the subsequent history of the Jews.   Chattel
slavery always trails along with itself a horrible
gang of barbarous accompaniments.   It never exists
without these.   These never appear in Jewish history.   Servants are never called *slaves*.   In every
other nation under heaven, where servants are made
slaves, they are sure to get the title: they are called
slaves.   The word servant never came to have a
degraded sense: the degraded sense which goes
along with the word slave, and which it inevitably
would have had, if servants had been slaves.   There
is no selling of servants.   There is no hunting of
fugitive slaves.   A civil police, to keep slaves in
subjection, never appears.   Slave auctions never
appear.   A slave traffic never appears.   Slave whip-
pings never appear.   Slave rebellions never appear.
The degraded slave class in society never appears.
In short, not one characteristic concomitant of chattel slavery ever appears in all the history of the
Jewish nation.   The relation did not exist among
them, and hence its concomitants are not to be
found.

5. So, if we go back and trace the history of the

servitude which descended in the Hebrew line from the Patriarchs who lived soon after the flood, we shall see that it must have been the free servitude of servant and master, and not the servitude of slave and owner. It came down from a period when chattel slavery was utterly impossible. It has been demonstrated that in the Patriarchal households it was free servitude. It is equally manifest that this same free servitude was the servitude which Moses found among the Jews, and to which he adapted his legislation. Precisely the same language is used in the Patriarchal history, and in the Mosaic code, in describing the servitude referred to. It is everywhere referred to as one and the same thing. In its origin it must have been the servitude whose relation is that of servant and master, and not the relation of slave and owner. In its descent along the line of Jewish history, there is no evidence that it ever became any thing else. This is the relation that is everywhere implied and contemplated in the legislation of the Mosaic code on the subject of servitude.

6. Hence, throughout the Old Testament, all trespass upon manhood rights, against servants, or any one else, all oppression, in every form, is denounced, and against it the most terrible judgments are threatened. The relation of servant and master is everywhere recognized and acknowledged as right and proper; but all injustice, all trespass upon the inalienable rights of man, all oppression, is rebuked and

denounced. This consists with the righteous relation of servant and master, but is totally inconsistent
with the relation of slave and owner. The relation
of servant and master consists with the preservation
of the full dignity of individual manhood and its
inalienable rights, intact and inviolable. The relation of slave and owner implies the subversion of
that dignity, and the destruction of those rights.
The relation of servant and master, therefore, is consistent with the denunciations of God's Word against
injustice and oppression : while the relation of slave
and owner will not admit of such denunciations.

7. The servitude, therefore, which is recognized
and sanctioned in the Patriarchal history, and of
which God testified that it was according to justice
and righteous judgment, (Gen. xviii: 19,) and that
servitude which Moses found among the Israelites,
which he regulated, and to which he adapted his
legislation—were one and the same thing: the servitude found in the righteous relation of servant and
master, and not that which is found in the relation
of slave and owner. To this latter relation Moses
devotes two verses, locating it, by a changeless record
and statute, among capital crimes.—(Ex. xxi: 16,
and Deut. xxiv: 7.)

8. In perfect harmony with all this, is the manner
in which the New Testament treats the same subject.
The righteous relation of servant and master appears
on almost every page, and is everywhere recognized
and sanctioned as right and proper. The other rela-

tion of slave and owner is left where the Old Testament leaves it: a capital crime. As such, Paul alludes to it once in 1 Tim., i: 10. It is said to be alluded to once in the Revelation. Whether it is elsewhere referred to in the New Testament, we do not know. This, then, is our conclusion: That the relation of unchattelized servitude runs through the Bible, and is everywhere recognized and sanctioned as a right and proper relation: that the relation of slave and owner is put in the catalogue of other gross crimes, and is dispatched in two or three verses and is there left.

CHAPTER XXIV.

REASON WHY SO FEW DIRECTIONS GIVEN TO MAS-
TERS AND SERVANTS—ON WHAT GROUND THESE
DIRECTIONS ARE GOOD FOR SLAVES AND SLAVE-
HOLDERS—SLAVEHOLDERS AND THE PRIMITIVE
CHURCHES.

THE reason why our Savior gives no specific directions to servants and masters, as such, and why so
few such directions are to be found anywhere in the
New Testament is, that the Bible everywhere exalts
the individual man, and always contemplates each
child of Adam, without respect of persons, as an
individual, legitimate son and heir of rationality and
immortality.   It goes back of society distinctions
and prejudices, and counts each soul a child and
creature of God.   It is no respecter of persons.   It
commands all people to call no man master; and it
commands them to honor all men.   What it says, is
addressed to every child of Adam, as God's creature,
for whom Christ died, and valued by him above all
price, as a rational, immortal soul.

And so the whole Bible is addressed to masters,
and the whole of it to servants.   There is not one
Bible for masters, and another for servants.   God's
Bible thinks just as highly of servants as it does of
masters, and places them both entirely on a level.

And the great object in what few specific directions are given, is to remind both servants and masters of this fact. Both are put under the same law, and the directions are concluded with the pregnant declaration that God is no respecter of persons.

And when the dust and cob-web gatherings of moth-eaten superstitions are fully wiped off from the Sacred page, the whole Bible is found to be one continued thundering cannonade against all trespass upon manhood rights. No particular, specific directions are really needed either for servants or masters, except to remind them that the great law of benevolence applies to them, belongs to them, and is the rule of action for them both. And, it is remarkable that this is exactly the character of the few directions that are given to them. Both are, alike, as we have seen, put under this great higher law: masters to obey it, by giving to the servants that which is just and equal; and servants to be under the direction of the masters, and render the service due cheerfully and uprightly. These facts characterize the directions in every case: the great object being to apply the great higher law of universal, impartial, unselfish good-will to the parties concerned. The relation of servant and master is right and proper: that relation is rightly sustained when sustained according to this higher law.

In regard to the other relation of slave and owner: (1.) It is an unrighteous, abnormal relation — a "violence" to all law and fitness not to be tolerated for a single moment. (2.) And secondly, all the directions given to masters and servants are in direct conflict with it: not adapted to that relation, nor designed for it. They can be applied to it only as you apply water to fire, to annihilate it.

The way is now prepared for us to see clearly the ground on which the directions given to servants are good also for slaves. Most of these directions are good for slaves, considered as servants with the super-added oppressions and abuses of slavery imposed upon them. While they continue in this condition, obedience is, undoubtedly, expedient and wise for them. But the slave is not under the least obligation to his master as *owner*. The ownership itself is contraband and wicked, and imposes not the least obligation upon the slave. Whatever of obligation there may be in the case, rests solely on the ground of expediency, and not at all on the ground of any thing due the slaveholder. In the relation of servant and master, the servant is under obligation to the master to render obedience on the ground of the relation he sustains to him as servant. In the relation of slave and owner, the slave is under no obligation whatever to render obedience to the owner on the ground of that relation. No slave under heaven owes the owner a single particle of duty, or service, or obedience, or respect, because he is a slave. This is a ground upon which obligation never grows. It may be expedient for the slave to render peaceful obedience: that is, the slave may be under obligation to *himself* to render obedience; he may be under obligation to the general good to do so. Just as a captive in a den of tigers might be under obligation to himself and the general good to "play 'possum," or do any thing else not in itself wrong, that might appear expedient. But the tiger's paws and jaws would impose no obligation upon him to be submissive. And just as a victim of the Romish Inquisition might be under obligation to himself and the general good to be passive and obedient, and to exhibit a Christian spirit. But he would be under no obligation to his tormentors to render either service or obedience. Neither is due to them, and they have no claim upon either. So of the slave in regard to his owner. He owes nothing to him as owner. If he were a free, voluntary servant, under pay, with acknowledged manhood, then he would owe obedience and service, on the ground of the relation which he sustained to his master. But this relation never covers the other relation of slave and owner: it never implies any portion of it, and never has any thing to do with it: it never carries any of its obligations over into it.

We can see, also, how these directions which are given to masters are good also for slaveholders. If slaveholders are to be contemplated as slaveholding masters, and their slaves as servants, then these directions apply, and they demand of the master to give unto his servants that which is just and equal. This instantly abolishes, annihilates, and puts a final end to chattel slavery. The first "just and equal" thing which the slaveholding master is to do in regard to his slave servants is, to cease at once and

20

forever to regard, or treat, or hold them as chattel slaves. He can not even begin to obey these directions without doing that. And that is immediate and complete emancipation and abolition to the full. In these directions, as applied to slaveholding masters, is to be found the only perfect abolition precept we have ever seen, except that one given from Moses in more general terms, namely, "Thou shalt love thy neighbor as thyself." If slaveholders go into the category of masters, and allow their slaves to come into the relation of servants, then the Divine Statute instantly meets them: "Masters give unto the servants that which is just and equal," instantly annihilating the slavery, and elevating both slaves and slaveholders into the righteous relation of servants and masters, with mutually acknowledged manhood, and with mutual respect for each other's rights as brethren of the same stock, and children of the same Father. This is God's legislation to slaveholders considered as masters. It is not civil legislation indeed, but moral legislation that is direct, perfect, and final. There is in it no dodging, no circumlocution, no softening of terms, no artifice to conceal the thing intended. It is simple, plain, personal, conclusive, and final.

And God's legislation to slaveholders, considered as slaveholders, is also as direct and conclusive. It has stood upon the Divine Record for all people to read and understand for more than three thousand years. "And he that stealeth a man, and selleth him, or if he be found in his hand, he shall surely be put to death."

We can also see what ground there is for supposing that slaveholders were admitted to the primitive
churches. There is just no ground at all. "But
were there not 'believing masters' in the primitive
churches?" Yes: but no believing slaveholders.
There is not a hint in the New Testament that slave-
owners were admitted to the primitive churches,
any more than there is that the bread used at the
Lord's Supper was made of spurred rye, and wet up
with a decoction of hen-bane. "Believing masters"
were admitted to the primitive churches, as they
always have been, and still are, all over Christen-
dom. Believing slave-owners constitute a class of
God and mammon worshipers not described in the
New Testament history. "Believing masters," who
have the true love of God and man in their hearts,
and who, consequently, fully acknowledge the equal
manhood of their servants, and give unto them, in
all respects, that which is just and equal, are always
proper subjects for admission to the Christian Church.
They make good members of it. Slave-owners constitute another class of people entirely. We have
never yet seen any evidence that there ever was
any room in the primitive churches for any such
people. Any master who was also a slave-owner, in
the modern property sense, who should come under
the rules, regulations, and teachings of the primitive
churches, must, of necessity, instantly drop his slave-
ownership, and be simply an honest master. The
door was altogether too narrow to admit the former,
but readily admitted the latter.

CHAPTER XXV.

SLAVERY AS A "SYSTEM," OR "INSTITUTION."

PEOPLE sometimes confuse their minds with the sound of the words "system" and "institution." Somehow, to them, the application of these words to slavery seems to change the whole aspect of it. They seem to have the impression that slavery, as a system, as an institution, in some way, and at some time, got imposed upon our Southern country much as the Almighty imposed night and day upon the earth. They unwittingly imagine that it is a sort of necessity, a domestic necessity, an institutional necessity, an organic necessity, so imposed that individual action and responsibility are mostly absorbed in the system. As a system, as an institution, they are unable to see how it can be touched, or how it can be managed, or how it can be got rid of, till its proper, providential moulting season regularly arrives, in due order.

But, pray, what is this system of slavery made up of? Why, it is all made up simply of *individual slaveholding*. It is nothing more nor less than combined, individual iniquity. There is no system about it, except multiplied, individual slaveholding. It is an institution of multiplied, individual crime, just as piracy is an institution on the high seas, just as licentiousness is an institution in our large cities, and just as theft was an institution among the Lacedæmonians. Any iniquity becomes an institution when a good many people perpetrate it, and seek to keep each other in countenance in the perpetration; and it becomes a decided institution when the civil law is laid under contribution to regulate it and sustain it. And this is all the system, all the institution, there is about slavery. As already intimated, it is nothing more nor less than individual slaveholding: it is all made up of individual slaveholding. It is imposed upon the slaveholder just as piracy is imposed upon the pirate, and just as licentiousness is imposed upon the rake. It is a deception to talk of it as a sort of irresponsible necessity of things, in the shape of an institution or system.

But multitudes of people greatly deceive themselves in their thinkings and sayings on this subject, by contemplating slavery as a system, or institution. A system is a soulless irresponsibility: so is an institution. Hence the Bible never speaks of slavery as a system. It never tells us how any form of iniquity, as a system, is to be managed. It deals with the individual man, the individual soul, and hence with individual iniquity. Amid the smoke and thunder of Sinai, and the fearful quakings of the mount beneath the tread of the Great Eternal, it speaks, face to face, to every child of Adam as an individual creature of God, capable of hearing for himself, "And he that stealeth a man, and selleth

him, or if he be found in his hand, he shall surely
be put to death!" Here is universal law, and yet
so couched as to be universally particular. The
precept is as broad as the universe, yet so individ-
ualized as to lay its firm grasp upon each single
soul. This is Bible wisdom. Its precepts sweep
the universe, and yet skip no man. It never fires
its thunders into promiscuous institutional heaps;
it never wastes its cannonades upon uninhabited old
castles, in the shape of soulless and irresponsible
systems, but always takes sure aim at the very
heart of personal and individual responsibility.
Hence it is, that no soul of man can escape its
omnipresent and personal thunders by drawing his
head into the dead shell of any system or institution. It is not the shell that the divine thunder is
leveled against; but the individual, living man in
the shell. Let no one, therefore, expect to find
either murder, or theft, or idolatry, or man-stealing,
alias slavery, or any other form of wickedness,
discussed in the Bible simply as a system. Its
wisdom is vastly better than that. It everywhere
assumes that individual and personal action is the
only thing that moral law has to do with. Hence,
as already said, its precepts sweep the universe, and
yet arraign each individual soul, face to face.

CHAPTER XXVI.

ORIGIN OF SLAVERY.

OF the origin of chattel slavery we have never yet seen any satisfactory account. Writers are apt to assume its existence, and to carry their assumption out upon much forbidden ground. It is manifest, however, that two things must have been true in regard to the origin of chattel slavery.

1. In the nature of the case, it could not have existed in the earliest times. It could not have existed in the family of Noah. It could not have existed for several generations following. People might have served each other in various ways and forms, but when the people were few, and the earth all lay common, they could not have enslaved each other. This is perfectly certain.

2. It is also manifestly true, that chattel slavery must have come into existence very gradually. It did not start into being at once, either as an individual thing, or as a system. As a system, it could have come into existence only with the *progress of society*. The process of its development must have been gradual, and something after the following order.

At first, after the flood, as social beings, and necessarily dependent, in many respects, upon each

other, individuals would, in various ways, do service
for each other. Mutual assistance belongs, of necessity, to all human society. The Hebrew word that
means *servant* can be distinctly traced directly back
to this sort of mutual assistance which individuals
rendered to each other in the earliest times. Its
first meaning, in the verbal form, is simply to labor,
or to do something. It meant, next, to do something
for another. Service to each other belongs to the
very existence of human society: and hence, servitude, in this free and honorable sense, is found in
connection with human society as far back as history
can be traced. As the race multiplied, after the
flood, they would form distinct and separate families
or households. These families would enlarge and
become tribes, or clans, or, if you please, compound
households, like that of Abraham. This would give
rise to Patriarchal government; for government of
some sort there must have been. But these tribes,
or, more properly, compound households, with Patriarchal rulers at the head, were not like little states
in modern times: but were enlarged households, consisting largely of kinsfolks, with other individuals
and families not so nearly related, associated with
them. Such association, under one Patriarchal head,
would involve service and subjection: a mixed service and subjection, partly family and partly governmental. Each tribe, or household, both as individuals and as a whole, would have numerous wants to
be supplied. They would need to be marshalled for
self-defense: for we are to remember all along that

human beings are a fallen race, and that selfishness reigns wherever they go. Being thus thrown together in tribes, or embryo nations, the various elements, offices, relations, and services of organized society would be gradually developed. The headman, or chief, would soon be a king, standing out with his own particular family and special friends, by himself. Subordinate officers, clothed with more or less authority, would be needed to direct the affairs of the clan. Various kinds of employment would readily come to be separated, classified, and exalted into trades and professions. There would be trade and traffic with each other, and with other clans. There would be all sorts of service to be done: the Patriarch, or chief having, all the time, the oversight and control of the whole. And so the whole tribe or household would very naturally come to take the name of servants of the chief who was at the head. This would be the natural and necessary progress of things. But in all this there is nothing like chattel slavery. There is service, and, in that sense, servitude: but, as yet, chattel slavery is impossible. The individual members of the clan are bound together simply and only by considerations of mutual and personal interest. A single breath might scatter the whole, and there would be no remedy; as a gust of wind will scatter a swarm of bees. As the whole heavens are open to all the bees, to go whithersoever they list, and no spirting of water, or drumming of brass kettles and old tin pans can help it, so the whole earth was open to all the individuals of the tribe, to go where they pleased, and each one set up for himself, and nobody could hinder it.

In the progress of things, it would be an object with each clan-household, or tribe, to enlarge and strengthen itself. This might be accomplished in several ways.

1. Each tribe would multiply within itself, giving rise to a population called "sons of the house," or " the born in the house."

2. In the second place, it would seek to attach other persons and families to itself, either by persuasion or contract, from outside of its own circle. This contract was made with the persons and families themselves, and was, by no means, a buying of persons as property, in the modern sense. Neither was it a simple hiring of services: but a contract for attaching said persons to the tribal household. When the contract was completed, it attached the persons entering into it to the tribe, or household, to belong to it, to do service with and for it, and be subject to it, and have citizenship in it. Persons thus attached were called "bought-with-money servants."

3. Clans would seek enlargement, also, by conquest: either peaceably, by negotiation, or forcibly, by warfare. In the earlier times, such conquest, even by war, did not reduce the captives to a state of chattel slavery. It only secured them and their possessions to the conquering clan, as subjects and servants. The custom of reducing captives taken in war, and captive nations, to a state of slavery, arose

later. In Patriarchal times, captured persons and tribes were not reduced to slavery. They were united with the conquering tribe, and subjected to its control as members and servants, and not as chattel slaves.

As human society progressed, and clans and households enlarged into nations and kingdoms, and as laws and customs became more and more fixed, and the earth filled up with inhabitants, human selfishness, always keen-eyed, began to take advantage of this state of things, and rulers, as well as others, sought to use the ignorant and weaker for their own advantage. Along with the progress of society and nation-building, this trespass gradually progressed, till it absorbed the man and made him a beast of burden—a chattel slave. It was by a slow and long period of travail that chattel slavery was born. It gradually grew out of the primitive clan-servitude, which was wholly free and voluntary, and which was a necessity of early society.

Now, it is a remarkable fact, that, with the progress of nations, and of human society, chattel slavery appeared in all nations outside of the chosen seed of Abraham, the true Abrahamic nation. In Egypt, in Greece, in Rome, with the progress of those nations, chattel slavery got into existence, and extended, and became worse and worse, more and more complete trespass upon, and absorption of, manhood rights. It is only with the progress of nations in civilization that slavery can reach its full growth and strength of villainy. It comes into

existence from free, righteous servitude, by a gradual trespass upon manhood rights, till it absorbs the
whole.   Selfishness having the power, as naturally
proceeds to this result as the water in the rivers
proceeds to the ocean.   The germ of slavery is to
be found first in trespass upon manhood rights:
when this germ has grown and extended till it absorbs the manhood itself, you have the perfect, live
viper, clear and clean from the shell.   To accomplish
this, and to secure a strong after-growth, it needs
the help of the machinery of civil law—of civil law
in an enlightened age.   This was the history of
things in ancient Greece, and in ancient Rome.

But in the true Abrahamic family, the Israelitish
nation, separated by the Almighty from all other
nations, chattel slavery never existed as a system,
never existed as an individual practice, except as a
capital crime.   Servitude never advanced beyond
the free, righteous, Patriarchal type.   In all other
nations, servitude ran down into chattelhood, fruit-
ing out into the grossest systems of legalized slavery.
But in the chosen and separated Abrahamic family
it was restrained to the model of the Patriarchal
households, which God himself pronounced according
to justice and true judgment.

This notable result was secured by two great
influences.

1. Very much was done to secure this result by
the experience of the Jews in the Egyptian "house
of bondage," by which the Hebrew heart was effectually taught to know the heart of the stranger, and

the heart of the poor and powerless. To this ex-perience God often appeals in warning them against oppression. "Thou shalt neither vex a stranger, nor oppress him;" "for ye know the heart of a stranger, seeing ye were strangers in the land of Egypt." "Thou shalt love him as thyself."

2. This result was confirmed and made sure by the Mosaic code. This code found the free servitude of Patriarchal days in existence, as an elemental part of Jewish society. It found the compound Abrahamic household still in existence. By its legislation, adapted to this state of things, fully pro-tecting both servant and master, it forever fore-stalled, and effectually prevented, the existence of chattel slavery among the Jews, except as a crime, in the same sense as theft and adultery existed as crimes. This is a wonderful and significant fact. God's revelation to Moses killed both idolatry and slavery among the Jews. Both of these great abom-inations lived and flourished outside of the Jewish nation, but had no foothold within it, except as great crimes.

This is what became of slavery among the Jews. Many writers seem much puzzled to find out when slavery *ceased* among the Jews, and how there came to be none among them in the time of Christ. The truth is, it never existed among them. The Mosaic legislation in regard to servitude is not legislation about slavery, but about free servitude. This is the servitude, and not chattel slavery, which existed in the Patriarchal families, and this is the servitude,

and not chattel slavery, which descended in the Jewish nation.   The Hebrews carried no slavery down
into Egypt: they had none in Egypt: they carried
none out of Egypt: they had none in the wilderness:
they carried none with them into the land of Judea:
they never had any there, and hence our Savior
found none there to come in contact with.   The
Jewish nation stands alone in this respect.   All
other nations went right on in idolatry and oppression, in the shape of slavery and otherwise, grinding
the people under foot, and making a prey of them.
The Jews stand alone, kept from these abominations
by the wonderful sojourn in Egypt, and the still
more wonderful revelation of law and truth to
Moses.

This view of the case suggests the reason why the
Hebrew language had no specific word for *slave*,
and none for *slavery*.   Says Mr. Barnes: "The Hebrews did not make distinctions between the various
kinds of service with the accuracy of the Greeks."*
And why ?   We answer, because the *things* themselves
did not exist: and not because the Hebrews had not
sense enough to find words for what existed and
was common among them.   The Hebrew was not a
meager language.   It had more words in it than
modern learning has yet been able to find out the
meaning of.   It is not to be assumed that all modern
forms of servitude and slavery existed among the
Jews, as a matter of course, and that the reason
why they are not particularly described by specific

* Scriptural Views of Slavery, p. 68.

terms was the poverty of the Hebrew tongue. By no means. The presumption rather is, that not being thus referred to, and not having words to express them, they did not exist. The Latin had no word for *steamboat;* but who would think of attributing this to the poverty of the Latin language? No. The want of the word implies ignorance of the thing. Languages always keep pace with the wants of the people. When ideas, customs, arts, things exist, words will not be wanting to designate those ideas, customs, arts, and things. Languages always have words and specific phrases for that with which the people using the language are familiar. Poverty of ideas makes poverty of language.

Now, the Jews were a world by themselves—isolated, separated. They had plenty of words, specific and general, for all Hebrew ideas, customs, and things. Servitude, among them, never ran down into chattel slavery, and hence the idea of slavery was unfamiliar to Hebrew thought. The Hebrew mind never got sufficiently accustomed to slavery to be at the trouble of having any specific words to mean slave or slavery. Among the Greeks, and Romans, and other nations, servitude ran down, with the progress of civilization, into chattel slavery, and hence the abundance of specific terms in their languages to express it. The Jews, not having the thing, needed not the terms to express it, and so had none.

This view of the origin of servitude, and of slavery as growing out of it, also reveals the origin of the

singular ancient custom of *buying wives*. When a
man of one household wished to marry a woman of
another household, the transaction would remove the
woman from the household to which she properly
belonged. In the earliest times this would be a
serious loss. To compensate for this, in some measure, the man was obliged to pay a sum of money.
In those days persons, as members of the household,
and not as property in the modern sense at all,
were of the greatest value. To have children, and
to have servants to increase the family, was esteemed
an object of the greatest importance. To balance the
gain on one side, and compensate for the loss on the
other side, the man must pay money before the
transfer could be made. After a while, this came to
be the universal custom in marriages, even when no
transfer from one tribe to another was made. It
had no more to do with chattel slavery than modern courtships have, in which the money goes the
other way. But to take the later condition of wives
in heathen countries, which is not much better, if
any, than that of slaves, and carry it back, and
make it the origin of the custom of buying wives,
is putting the cart before the horse truly.

CHAPTER XXVII.

ONESIMUS.

ONE of the most marvelous literary wonders of modern times is the pro-slavery interpretation which has been so frequently given to Paul's Epistle to Philemon. Messrs. Conybeare and Howson have done the cause of slavery great service by the manner in which they have interpreted and treated this Epistle; for which they deserve, and doubtless will receive, the thanks of all man-robbers on both continents. Without blushing, they make Philemon a thoroughbred, modern slaveholder; Onesimus a miserable, "starving," runaway "slave," "dragged forth" by the Apostle from the "dregs and offal" of Canada refugee society, and "surrendered" by him to his "rich" Phrygian master, with all the dignity and pious obedience to the laws of the land becoming to the slave-hunting officials of American democracy. According to these authors, slaveholding and slave-catching are abundantly sanctified in this Epistle.

Now, we need not say that this appears to us to be both monstrous teaching, and monstrous perversion of the Divine Word. We think, most surely, that the evidence is totally wanting, either that Philemon was a slaveholder, or that Onesimus was his slave, or that St. Paul ever had any hand in "surrendering" fugitive slaves to their masters.

The following considerations will exhibit our reasons for thus thinking:

1. Onesimus is nowhere *called a slave*. Paul applies to him no other terms, or epithets, than such as he is accustomed to apply to himself, and to all Christians. He calls him a "servant," but never a *slave*. Since, therefore, Paul calls Onesimus a servant, and never a slave, the presumption is that he was a servant, and not a slave.

. 2. The supposition that Onesimus was a servant, and not a slave, satisfactorily meets all the conditions of the case, while the supposition that he was a slave, and Philemon a slaveholder, and Paul a slave-catcher, involves numerous very unhappy inconsistencies and contradictions.

(1.) It is not at all probable that a poor Phrygian slave would flee from his owner so far as Onesimus was found from Philemon. It appears, from the Epistle itself, as well as from Col. iv: 9, that Onesimus had lived with Philemon at Colosse, and that he had departed from him to Rome, where he was converted to the Christian faith, through the instrumentality of Paul. Now, Colosse was nearly or quite a thousand miles from Rome, in a straight line. The journey, by land and water, would have required twelve or fifteen hundred miles of travel: by land wholly, more than two thousand miles. It is extremely unlikely that a runaway slave, in those times, would have undertaken any such journey as that. This improbability is greatly increased by the fact that, of all places on the face of the earth, Rome was, at that time, the worst for a fugitive slave. Nowhere else were slaves so completely degraded and trodden under foot. A fleeing to Rome, as a runaway slave, in the days of Onesimus, was much like the fleeing of a mödern, New Jersey slave to New Orleans. We are decidedly of the opinion that Onesimus had too much wit to undertake, as a runaway slave, any such expedition as that.

But, as a free servant—Philemon's private secretary, for aught appears—a man owning himself, and master of his own affairs and pocket, it was as suitable for Onesimus to "depart" to Rome, as for any one else. If he was an old bachelor, as was probably the case, it was highly suitable for him to "depart" "from" Philemon and his household! At any rate, he might as well "depart" "from" *him* as from any one else.

(2.) The manner in which Paul alludes to Onesimus, in the Epistle to the Colossians, utterly forbids the notion that he was a fugitive slave. Col. iv: 7–9—"All my state shall Tychicus declare unto you, who is a beloved brother, and a faithful minister and fellow-servant in the Lord: Whom I have sent unto you for the same purpose, that he might know your estate, and comfort your hearts; With Onesimus, a faithful and beloved brother, who is one of you. They shall make known unto you all things which are done here." Among the few honorable names of leading and prominent ones in the primitive

church worthy of transmission to posterity, Tychicus and Onesimus stand associated together, as
"faithful and beloved," upon the Inspired page.
"They," as it seems, were commissioned by the
great Apostle with messages to the Church in the
city of Colosse, and to make known unto said Church
all things which were done at Rome.   They were
both, alike, "sent" on this errand by the Apostle, to
the Church at Colosse.   They seem to have prose-
cuted the journey together, bearing the Epistle to
the Colossians: Onesimus carrying, also, a special
epistle to Philemon.   Now, who can believe that the
great and learned Apostle of the Gentiles would
have commissioned a miserable, vagabond, run-away
slave, who, not long before, as we are told, had fled
from Colosse, "a thief," to bear messages and tidings
to the Church in the great, and wealthy, and popu-
lous* city of Colosse?   And who can suppose that
the Church would have received such a messenger?
Slaveholding churches have mightily changed since
those days, else such a supposition is preposterous.
But, dropping the baseless fancies of pro-slavery interpreters, that Onesimus was the slave of Philemon,
a thief, and a vagabond, and contemplating him as a
gifted and accomplished person, whom Philemon had
employed in some service not mentioned, and who
had departed from him to Rome, either on business,
or from motives of curiosity or pleasure, and who had
been converted there through the instrumentality of
Paul, we have before us a suitable messenger from

* Xenophon and Herodotus.

Paul and his friends at Rome to the Church in the city of Colosse. All the more suitable and acceptable, from the fact that he had been well known in Colosse as a skeptical fellow, whose *unprofitableness* to Philemon, in the Gospel, was well known in the Church.

(3.) The manner in which Paul speaks of Onesimus, in the Epistle to Philemon, is utterly inconsistent with the notion that he was the man-chattel of Philemon. "Whom I would have retained with me."—V. 13. What business had Paul to think of keeping another man's property? "Why, Paul, the Apostle, might as well have retained a bundle of bank bills, or a cask of Spanish dollars belonging to Philemon. What! Paul, the Apostle, who was of such proud, incorruptible, and almost superfluous honesty, that he would not even receive a farthing for his preaching, but, at this very time, had his hands roughened and chapped with the toil of tent-making for his daily bread; . . . . Paul, who had written: Let him that stole, steal no more; Paul, this Apostle Paul, put his hand, as it were, into Philemon's pocket, and steal from him at least a thousand dollars—detain from him the most sacred thing in the shape of property on his plantation? Even the *intention* was burglary." . . . . .
"Paul" should "have said: Whom I would *not* have retained on any consideration whatever, and never thought of doing such a thing, but have advertised you, brother Philemon, that you might prove property, pay its charges, and take it away."*

* Dr. Cheever

(4.) "Thou, therefore, receive him, that is, mine own bowels."—V. 12. "Receive him as myself."—V. 17. 'Indeed, father Paul, you ought to be ashamed of that: Onesimus is my property, to buy and sell, to work, to whip, to breed for the market, to do the service of a slave. God forbid that I should put the great Apostle of the Gentiles to such uses as these.'

(5.) "If he hath wronged thee, or oweth thee aught, put that on mine account."—V. 18. This clearly implies that Onesimus was competent to contract debts. It does not imply that he actually did owe Philemon any thing. As a free servant, he might have owed Philemon either service on unexpired time for which he had been paid, or money borrowed, or due for property. Paul's confidence in Onesimus' conversion, as being genuine, was so strong that he was perfectly willing to become responsible to Philemon for any debts that Onesimus might have contracted. But all this implies that Onesimus was his own man, and not the slave of any one.

(6.) The allusion in the 16th verse is wholly inconsistent with the relation of slave and owner. "Not now as a servant, but above a servant, a brother beloved, especially to me, but how much more unto thee, both in the flesh, and in the Lord?" In this verse Paul recognizes Onesimus as "a brother beloved," to himself, in the Lord; and as "a brother beloved," to Philemon, both "in the flesh, and in the Lord." He was brother to Philemon both in the flesh, and in the Lord. He was brother in the

Lord to Philemon, by conversion, and only after conversion. He was brother to him in the flesh, before conversion, and without reference to conversion. Now, to suppose that this refers to the relation which Onesimus sustained to Philemon, as his slave, is sufficiently absurd. It is certainly an odd thing under the sun to make the phrase, " brother in the flesh," synonymous with the word "slave." Surely, this can not be the sense.

Some suppose that Onesimus was actually, by birth, a younger brother of Philemon. If Philemon was the first-born, and Onesimus a younger brother, according to the universal custom of ancient times, the place of Onesimus, in the household, would be that of subjection and service to his elder brother, who would be the acknowledged lord of the household. Onesimus appears much more like one of those independent youngsters who dislike the control of an older brother, and who are every way unprofitable in the household, than like a chattel slave. But this is largely conjecture, and can not be demonstrated as fact. Nevertheless, it can not be proved to be false.

But it must be that the phrase, "brother in the flesh," indicates, at least, that Onesimus sustained some relation to Philemon very similar to that of brother by blood relationship. This language can not possibly mean less than this. But this excludes totally all slavery. If Onesimus was Philemon's brother in the flesh, in this sense he could not have been his slave. He may have been an adopted

brother: he may have been in Philemon's service
so long as to have become entitled to this cogno-
men: he may have been an orphan, taken into the
household in early life. But to describe a slave of
a rich Phrygian master as "a brother in the flesh,"
is a mockery in language in which we do not believe
St. Paul ever indulged.

3. The pro-slavery interpretation of the Epistle
to Philemon is wholly a gratuity. Is it said that
Paul "sent" Onesimus to Philemon? In like manner it is said that he "sent" Tychicus to the church
at Colosse. They were both "sent" together, and
on the same errand. But this did not imply that
either of them was a slave. Does Paul call Onesimus a "servant?" This no more implies that he
was a slave than it does that he was a land agent,
or a horse-jockey. Paul calls himself a "servant,"
and he was a *bona-fide* servant when he made tents at
Corinth under master Aquila. Did Paul say to Philemon, "But without thy mind would I do nothing;
that thy benefit should not be, as it were, of necessity,
but willingly?" If Onesimus was, after his conversion, a valuable friend, companion, and helper in the
Gospel, which plainly appears from what Paul has
written, and if Philemon had a prior claim to his
friendship and help, on the ground of past acquaintance, as is clearly manifest, there was good reason
why Paul should speak as he did, without lugging
in slavery for an explanation. So of every word
and phrase in this Epistle. A pro-slavery interpretation is needless, and wholly gratuitous.

4. "No longer as a servant, but above a servant." Not as though Paul regarded the condition of a servant a degraded one. Not as though Paul's mind was full of modern pro-slavery prejudice in regard to laboring people, and unbrotherly notions as to caste, and such like abominations. "Above a servant." Before his conversion, Onesimus was simply a servant, an unconverted sinner, a child of wrath, a servant of the devil. He was a brother man, to be sure, but an unconverted sinner, with whom Philemon could have no familiar friendship, that is, no such friendship as is implied in the fellowship of the Gospel. Being converted, he comes at once into the new, sacred, and high relationship of a Christian brother, a blood-bought fellow-heir of eternal life. He is now to be received into this new brotherhood equality, which there is in Christ, vastly above a mere servant in the household. We do not regard this as direction to Philemon to emancipate Onesimus from slavery, but to receive him as a Christian brother, in the fullest sense.

5. "Which in time past was to thee unprofitable." How? Not because he did not work hard enough as a slave, as some of the commentators, in their multiplied wisdom, seem to indicate; not in any pecuniary sense, for there is no particular allusion to that, but in a moral and spiritual sense. We do not think that Paul was troubled, on Philemon's behalf, because Onesimus had not been driven hard enough, as a slave, to come up to the demands of the divine law. We do not believe that divine

22

inspiration ever cared to express sympathy of that sort.

Probably Onesimus was a skeptical fellow, of a shrewd mind, whom Philemon did not understand how to meet, and who greatly tried and annoyed him, both by rejecting the Gospel and caviling against it. It seems that he remained impenitent and unyielding, proof against the prayers, and arguments, and exhortations of Philemon, until the divine logic of the profound and philosophic Apostle of the Gentiles met him at Rome. As Paul, his spiritual father, had been "injurious," before his conversion, and was plucked as a brand from the burning, and made a chosen vessel to carry the great salvation to the Gentiles, so Onesimus, the "beloved" spiritual "son," was, "in time past," "unprofitable," both in the household of Philemon and in the city of Colosse; but afterward, through the abounding grace of God, became "profitable," both in Rome and in Colosse. The "son" was so much like the father, that Paul could well say, "*Receive him as myself.*"

6. "But now profitable to thee and to me." Not in the slave sense, not as Paul's shoe-black at Rome, not to do the tugging and lifting for Paul, so that he could sit all day long in his rocking-chair and sing Psalms—but profitable to help in the Gospel. Being converted from his ungodliness to the Christian faith, Onesimus would no longer be a hindrance, but a help, in the Gospel, both to Paul and to Philemon. This the Apostle urges as a reason why Philemon

should receive him. A good and sufficient reason truly, infinitely more becoming the great Apostle and his Christian brother, Philemon, than the commentary-fancy that Onesimus, as a slave, had not worked hard enough, and earned, by the sweat of his brow, money enough for his owner!

As Onesimus had been unprofitable and a trouble to Philemon in time past, he was, doubtless, glad to get rid of him. Paul exhorts Philemon to receive Onesimus on the ground of his conversion, and because he will now no longer be a trouble, but a help in the Gospel. As a skeptical, caviling, ungodly servant, Philemon was, doubtless, glad of his departure: and had, probably, made up his mind that he would have nothing more to do with him. Paul, understanding how things were, as was fit, addressed to Philemon, and *to the Church in his house,* (v. 2,) this Epistle, to introduce Onesimus as a *Christian brother.* How could Onesimus have appeared before the Colossian Church with the messages which Tychicus and himself were commissioned to bear to that Church, (Col. iv: 9,) without such letter of introduction, having been known before only as "unprofitable," and opposed to the Gospel of Christ?

And, after his conversion, of course he himself would desire to go back to his old master and friend, and communicate the good news, repair any wrong which he had done, pay up all old scores, and help in the Gospel. Paul beseeches Philemon thus to receive him; offering to become security for Onesimus, either till he could make payment, or that he

might be immediately released from all entangle-
ments, in preaching the Gospel.

Paul had so much confidence in the sound conversion of Onesimus that, at first, he proposed to engage him to help in the Gospel with himself, at
Rome.   But it was, manifestly, important for him to
return to Colosse and repair all wrongs, make confession, and do justice to his old master first.   Paul
could not, therefore, well retain him without Philemon's consent.   Therefore, to clear the way for his
after usefulness in the Church of Christ, he "sent"
him back as a brother beloved, to repair all wrong,
pay up his debts, make confession, and set every-
thing right.   Such, as we understand it, is the spirit
of this Epistle to Philemon.

CHAPTER XXVIII.

BRIEF EXAMINATION OF SOME ANTI-SLAVERY VIEWS.

SEC. 1.—*Unhappy Translation of some portions of the Bible that relate to Servitude.*

ONE of the greatest and most ruinous mistakes of modern literature is the pro-slavery coloring which the venerable translators gave to certain passages in our English Bible. That these passages have a pro-slavery cast, can not be denied: that they ought not to have, is equally certain. Readers of our English Bible almost universally get the impression that there was chattel slavery in the Patriarchal households, and that some sort of provision was made for its continued existence among the Jews. The translation is calculated to produce that impression. Whether this was designed, on the part of the translators, we do not pretend to say. True to the original Hebrew, which had no single word for "*slave*" or "*slavery*" in it—they never use these words in the translation. But the translation itself looks just as if the translators did understand that slavery existed in the Patriarchal families, and was the subject of legislative regulation and sanction in the Mosaic code. In numerous passages they make an apparent distinction between "*servant*" and "bond-servant," when no such distinction exists in the original Hebrew. A single example, out of many that might be adduced, will sufficiently illustrate this. "Let thy servant abide instead of the lad, a bondman to my Lord."—Gen. xlvi: 33. Here, the Hebrew for "*servant*" and "*bondman*" is one and the same word. In the same way, the word "*sell*" is so managed in our translation as to make distinctions looking toward slavery, which have no foundation in the original Hebrew. One example will suffice: "If thy brother that dwelleth by thee, be waxen poor, and be *sold* unto thee."—Lev. xxv: 39; verse 47: "If a sojourner or a stranger wax rich by thee, and thy brother that dwelleth by him wax poor, and *sell himself* unto the stranger or sojourner by thee." Here, also, the Hebrew for the words "*sold*" and "*sell himself*" is one and the same word: the proper sense of which, in both cases is—"*sell himself*."

This mistake in the rhetorical and logical tone of various passages in our English translation has been most fruitful in errors and mischievous results. It is the fountain-head of an immense pro-slavery corruption in the literature of the age. Our commentaries, our lexicons, our Bible dictionaries, our school books, our newspapers—are more or less tinged with this same vicious coloring. Bible sanction of, or winking at, slavery, derived from a mistaken, pro-slavery translation of the true, original anti-slavery Bible—runs through our English literature. It is a base habit of our literature to assume that there is some sort of divine connivance at slavery, in the Word of God.

This is a great evil under the sun. Our children, our college students, our people in the mass, old and young, are thus covertly and silently, but effectually, constantly taught erroneous, pro-slavery doctrines, and that, too, with divine sanction.

This same mistake has run into the anti-slavery creed of many anti-slavery men, and has greatly marred and paralyzed the moral force of the creed, and weakened the moral position of the men who hold the creed. Both the creed and the men need to be purged of this weakness.

SEC. 2.—*The Bible Argument of Dr. Hopkins: its Strength: its Weakness: its Inconsistency.*

One of the boldest and ablest of the early anti-slavery advocates in this country was the redoubtable Dr. Hopkins, of Newport. He maintained, unequivocally and strongly, that the owning of slaves was SIN against God and man, and, as such, he poured out a vehement stream of eloquent and powerful argument and malediction against it. In this position, in itself impregnable, lay his strength on this subject. But his otherwise mighty strength against chattel slavery was greatly weakened by a single, fundamental, mistaken admission. That admission was, that this intrinsic and great sin against God and man had, in past ages, and in peculiar circumstances, received God's sanction. Why should not people be slow to admit the sinfulness of American chattel slavery, when those who, in one breath denounced it as such, in the very next, admitted that Jewish chattel slavery, a few years gone by, had received the divine approbation? And why should there not be endless jangle among lesser theologians on the question, Whether chattel slavery is sin *per se*, if the great giant in theology had pronounced it really such, if not in terms, and yet had admitted and expressly taught that God had, at one time, given his direct sanction to this "sin *per se?*" Dr. Hopkins evidently saw, very clearly, that the owning of human beings, as property,- was sin against God and man. On this ground he justly denounces it, and calls upon all slaveholders at once to emancipate their slaves. Clear, and good, and right, and strong, so far.

But here the Bible pro-slavery objector encounters him. The Doctor courageously sticks to his position, and undertakes to defend the Bible. In this defense he commits a fatal mistake. He makes an admission that has already cost Christianity and the cause of human liberty too dear. Without thorough examination of Patriarchal customs and Mosaic legislation, he followed the pro-slavery bias of our English translation of the Bible, and undertook the hopeless task of giving good reasons why God gave the Jews the privilege of committing this particular sin! All honor to the clearness of his head in regarding chattel slavery as gross moral wrong: all honor to his moral courage in denouncing it as such: all honor to his faith and piety in defending the Bible: but it is not necessary for all the world everlastingly to follow his grievous mistake in this latter effort.

We are very anxious that the reader should understand precisely what this mistake is: as it has been copied and repeated, times without number, and is still put forth in high places as sound, antislavery orthodoxy. It is to be found in the following assumption, in Dr. Hopkins's own words: "And it was right for them [the Jews] to make bond-servants of the nations round them, they having an express permission to do it from Him who has a right to dispose of all men as he pleases. God saw fit, for wise reasons, to allow the people of Israel thus to make and possess slaves."* For this supposed permission to the Jews "to make and possess slaves," he gives explanation as follows: "God gave many directions and laws to the Jews which had no respect to mankind in general; and this under consideration has all the marks of such a one. There is not any thing in it, or relating to it, from whence can be deduced the least evidence that it was designed to be a regulation for all nations, through every age of the world, but every thing to the contrary." He illustrates and enforces his development of the "wise reasons" why God allowed the people of Israel "thus to make and possess slaves," by bringing forward the command given to the Jews to destroy the nations of Canaan for their

* Hopkins on Slavery: Congregational Board of Publication, p. 564.

23

iniquities. President Edwards, the younger, and multitudes of writers since, have pursued, substantially, the same course of argumentation. It is fairly the fashion for anti-slavery writers who would escape the charge of infidelity and ultraism, to make the same assumption, and to render the same explanation. But this course of explanation and argumentation will not bear examination.

1. In the first place, this view of the subject entirely fails to satisfy the public conscience. Many accept it as the best that can be done in the case, who are, nevertheless, far from being satisfied with it. Others, in large numbers, are totally dissatisfied with it, and, finding nothing better, seek to escape from the whole difficulty by rejecting the Bible altogether, as of divine authority. It can not be denied that this identical view of the subject has pushed multitudes clear over into the dark slough of infidelity. Others still, whose orthodoxy is stronger, stoutly determine that this explanation of the matter shall, per force, be fully satisfactory, who yet secretly wish there was a better one. They do solemnly think that if Dr. Hopkins, and other great and good doctors have been satisfied therewith, they *ought* to be: but they are not altogether, notwithstanding. It does not suit the public conscience to admit, either expressly or impliedly, that Mosaic divine inspiration was less luminous, less correct, and somewhat looser in regard to principles and practices than divine inspiration of a later period. Divine light ought to be as reliable

in one age of the world as in another. It is deeply felt, in the public conscience, that that is indeed tough revelation from God, which constituted the whole Hebrew people a nation of slave-makers and slaveholders, at their own discretion, as long as they should continue to be a nation at all!

2. In the second place, we venture to affirm that the main assumption in this explanation is wholly false. We deny, outright, that God ever gave to the Patriarchs, or to Moses, or to anybody else, the right, or the sufferance either to make or to hold slaves. We believe it to be an entire mistake to suppose that God ever gave any such right to any human being. We think that this can be fully shown.

3. But this explanation of Old Testament sanction of chattel slavery has other fatal objections. It involves principles inconsistent with the known character of God, and the established laws of the divine government. We propose to show this, by showing that the parallel examples adduced to illustrate and fortify this explanation are totally irrelevant. The strongest of these examples is the command given to the Jews to destroy the inhabitants of the land of Canaan for their iniquities. This command is quoted as similar and parallel to the supposed command given to the Jews to make and possess slaves. Let us examine the two, side by side, and see, if we can, wherein they are alike, and wherein they differ.

There are several circumstances connected with the command given to the children of Israel for the destruction of the Canaanites, that need to be distinctly and carefully noted. (1.) This was an *express, divine command.* It was not a dubious conclusion, inference, or guess from something else, but a direct and clearly-uttered command from Almighty God. (2.) The *reason* for it is distinctly and expressly stated. The iniquity of the inhabitants of the land had become ripe for their destruction. They were to be destroyed directly, and by special command, *for their wickedness,* just as other nations were to be, and have been, destroyed providentially, for the same reason. Their destruction was national, for national crimes. It was to be special and direct, in obedience to a special and direct order from God. (3.) Hence, the *principle involved* in this command is a common and fixed principle of God's government. It is neither exclusively an old-dispensation principle, nor a new-dispensation principle, but a great principle of the divine government for all time and all nations. God does destroy nations providentially for their crimes. He has done it in ages gone by: and he has not finished doing it yet: and, doubtless, he will not cease doing it as long as nations continue to forget God and become hopelessly wicked. This is, universally, the order of the divine government. Individual criminals also, are, ever have been, and ever ought to be, punished under the administration of human government, which is a part of the divine government. The *principle*, then, of this particular command given to the Jews to destroy the nations of

Canaan for their iniquities, belongs, as a matter of fact, to God's government, and is good and righteous for all times and peoples. (4.) Furthermore, being a special command, it was *definite*, stating and limiting exactly what was to be done. The objects of the command were definitely described. The executioners were to use no discretionary power. They were to do a particular thing, and then stop. The command was to be immediately executed and finished. They were to obey the special order fully and promptly, but not one particle of discretionary power or privilege was given them. Now, in all this, there is neither break nor flaw. There is nothing new, peculiar, or strange.

Bearing these things in mind, let us look at the supposed command given to the Jews "to make and possess slaves," which is said to be similar to the command we have just been considering. This command, if found anywhere, occurs in the twenty-fifth chapter of Leviticus, verses 44–46, and is as follows: "Both thy bondmen and thy bondmaids, which thou shalt have, shall be of the heathen that are round about you; of them shall ye buy bondmen and bondmaids. Moreover, of the children of the strangers that do sojourn among you, of them shall ye buy, and of their families that are with you, which they begat in your land: and they shall be your possession. And ye shall take them as an inheritance for your children after you, to inherit them for a possession: they shall be your bondmen forever." This is the particular command which has been supposed to give to the Jews the special and exclusive right to hold property in man: and which has been understood to be parallel with the command given to the Jews to destroy the nations of Canaan for their iniquities. But this parallelism is entirely imaginary.

(1.) In the first place, there is nowhere in the Sacred Record the smallest hint that the Jews were permitted, or directed, to procure "bondmen and bondmaids," which the Doctor interprets "to make and possess slaves" from the "heathen," or nations round about them, *as a punishment for their crimes.* The assignment of this reason is all guess-work. The Record itself gives no such reason. The direction in these verses is wholly unqualified. Prof. Bush interprets the phrase, "the heathen that are round about you," as referring to "the heathen then inhabiting the countries round about the Holy Land, but not to the Canaanites, whom they were required to destroy." This direction, then, whatever its true import may be, relates to "heathen," or, more properly, *nations*, in regard to whose punishment God had said nothing, and given no directions to the Jews. The reason given by Dr. Hopkins, namely: that the Jews were "to make and possess slaves" of the heathen round about them, as a punishment for their crimes, is purely imaginary.

(2.) In the next place, the direction in these verses *gives universal, discretionary power* to those to whom they were addressed, *as to the objects* of that direction. These objects are not defined at all, except by the word "heathen," which is a general term, signifying simply "foreigners." They might be deserving of punishment, or they might not be. They might even be a Ruth, mother of Messiah. But who can believe that God gave to each individual of the Jewish nation a divine permission to constitute himself a special minister of divine vengeance, to execute judgment at discretion upon whomsoever of the heathen round about he might please, by · reducing· them to chattel slaves, as a punishment for their crimes; thus opening and establishing, for the benefit of the Jews, a general inland slave-trade outright, to all generations of the Jewish people? But you must believe this, to its fullest extent, if the direction in these verses which we are considering be interpreted so as to give the Jews the right "to make and possess slaves" of the heathen round about them, for the punishment of their crimes. The direction in these verses, mark, is not limited as to time: it is not limited as to its particular objects: it is not limited even as to the character of the objects. If it refers to "making and possessing slaves," it constitutes a living and perpetual right to the Jews, for all coming time, "to make and possess slaves" of foreigners, except the Canaanites, at their own individual discretion, whether deserving of punishment or totally undeserving. This represents God as giving orders to the Jews, at the very outset of their national history, to destroy the Canaanites absolutely, and to make slaves of all the rest of the world! Believe this who can?

(3.) Again, *the principle* involved in this interpretation is totally inadmissible in the divine government.   That principle, remember, if we take the
Divine Record as it stands, is discretionary power
"to make and possess slaves" of foreigners, without
any reference to the punishment of crime, or the
character of the persons so enslaved: or, if we
adopt the groundless assumption of Dr. Hopkins, it
is general, discretionary power "to make and possess slaves" of foreigners, for the punishment of
their crimes.   In the former case, the principle is
intrinsically unjust, and at war with the great fundamental principles of the government of God—the
principles of righteousness and truth.   It was never
good for the Jews, and it never can be good for
either Jews or Gentiles.   The principle involved in
the command to destroy the nations of Canaan for
their crimes, and because their crimes had made
them ripe for such destruction, was a good and
sound one; applicable to all times and people, constantly acted upon in the providence of God, and in
the administration of human government.   But the
principle involved in this supposed command to the
Jews, "to make and possess slaves," at will, of the
nations around them, is utterly base and unrighteous, in direct conflict with the law of universal
brotherhood, and admissible to neither Jew nor
Gentile.   The two things are about as parallel as
the spokes of a cart-wheel—the more you expand
and extend them, the further they separate from
each other.

In the latter case, also, we venture to affirm, that *the chattelizing of human beings is altogether an inadmissible form of punishment for crime.* Criminals, even, have some rights. They have the right to be punished as rational creatures of God. Devils, even, have this right. Indeed, all right of punishment is based upon actually possessed and acknowledged rationality. All criminals have the right to be regarded as *criminal men,* and not as brute cattle. They, of necessity, forfeit many privileges; and when the crime is a capital one, even life itself; but they never forfeit their own characteristic, rational creatureship, which God himself has given them as their changeless and everlasting birthright. They never can deserve ill-will, or abuse, or beastly degradation, from any being. The punishment of confinement, of hard labor, of death, may be laid upon them properly and justly: but we protest that the chattelizing of human beings is a degrading abuse of absolute manhood which does not lie within the circle even of proper punishment for crime. Hence it was not a slip of Moses's pen that he forgot to annex to this passage of Scripture from Leviticus, which we have been considering, as the reason for what is therein arranged, that "the heathen" were to be punished for their iniquities by being thus made slaves of by the Jews at discretion. There were great fundamental reasons why Moses would never put two such things together: and it is certainly a great marvel to our mind, that so many great and good men have so coolly put such things together, and have so confidently quoted the command for the destruction of the Canaanites as illustrating and confirming the illegitimate alliance. Bad logic never put two worse bedfellows upon the same bedstead.

It is plain, therefore, that this Hopkinsian exposition of old-dispensation slavery is inadmissible. It makes a fatal mistake in admitting and assuming that *chattel slavery* had a tolerated existence in the Patriarchal households, and was made a subject of legislative regulation and sufferance in the Mosaic code. This is the common mistake of regarding the free, righteous servitude of the Patriarchal households, and of the Mosaic code, as chattel slavery. The explanation built upon this mistake is, as we have seen, open to fatal objections. The assumption is a groundless one, and the explanation is a bad one and both ought to be abandoned.

CHAPTER XXIX.

BRIEF CRITICISMS UPON SOME OTHER ANTI-SLAVERY VIEWS.

DURING the last few years several attempts have been made to answer the inquiry: "How does the Bible treat slavery?" These attempts have elicited much important truth: but some of them have been signal examples of unfortunate statement and bad logic. They have dishonored the Bible, and weakened the hands of anti-slavery men. Some of these mistaken views have been widely disseminated under the sanction of great and honored names; and, for the want of better views, they have been extensively received.

Certain writers, of high authority in other matters, maintain that it is the policy of the Bible to treat slavery indirectly, covertly seeking its overthrow as an evil, by laying down great principles designed to work its extinction gradually, and seeking, meanwhile, to regulate and restrain it. They say that the writers of the Bible—Old Testament and New—were quite "familiar" with slavery; that "they do not often refer to" it; that they "nowhere represent slavery as a divine institution," and "nowhere approve of it or give it their sanction;" that they "lay down truths and principles which are directly opposed to all slavery;" that while the inspired writers "suffered" the existence of slavery, they sought "to regulate and restrain" it—not "aiming" "at the ultimate extinction of slavery" "suddenly, and by positive enactment—but gradually." They argue that this was the policy of the Mosaic code, of the old prophets, of Jesus Christ, and of the apostles, in regard to slavery.

This view of Bible treatment of slavery, as the reader will at once see, is all necessitated by the mistake that the legislation of the Bible concerning free, or common servitude, was legislation concerning chattel slavery. Take this mistake from underneath this view, and the view itself, with all its argument, is no longer needed.

This view assumes that the servitude of the Patriarchal households was chattel slavery. This, as we have seen, is an entire mistake.

This view assumes that the legislation of the Mosaic code concerning free servitude was legislation concerning chattel slavery. This, also, is wholly a mistake. As we have seen, chattel slavery had no place in the Mosaic code, except as a crime to be punished.

 _ This view assumes, also, that the special instructions of the New Testament in regard to servants and masters are instructions concerning slaves and their owners. This, too, is all mistake.

The *argument* involved in this view is also sadly at fault. This whole argument proceeds on the assumption that the legislation of the Bible, and especially of the Mosaic code, concerning common servitude, assumed to be concerning chattel slavery —is merely regulating and restraining legislation respecting a known and admitted evil, for its ultimate removal.

But this assumption, so freely and unwittingly taken for granted by so many writers, is altogether a groundless one. As a matter of fact, the laws in the Mosaic code - respecting common servitude, which are supposed, in the argument under consideration, to refer to chattel slavery—are positive enactments: instituting, fully approving, and sanctioning that which is enacted. They bear no marks of enactments for the mere sufferance, restriction and regulation of that which is the subject-matter of enactment. They are direct, positive, institutive. Any individual, by looking, can see that this is the character of the enactment found in Ex. xxi: 2–6, and which has been supposed to refer to the enslavement of Jews by their brethren; and which does so refer, as much as any passage in the Mosaic code. Just read the passage, kind reader, and see if you can find any thing else in it but direct, positive enactment, giving full sanction to what is therein enacted. "If thou buy an Hebrew servant, six years he shall serve; and in the seventh he shall go out free for nothing. If he came in by himself, he shall go out by himself; if he were married, then his wife shall go out with him. If his master have given him a wife, and she have borne him sons or daughters: the wife and her children shall be her master's, and he shall go out by himself. And if the servant shall plainly say, I love my master, my wife, and my children, I will not go out free : Then his master shall bring him unto the judges; he shall also bring him to the door, or unto the door-post: and his master shall bore his ear through with an awl, and he shall serve him forever." Here, manifestly, provision is made for the perpetuity of that which is the subject of this enactment. It is not contemplated as an evil at all : it is cut off, by the terms of the statute itself, from the reach of any " great truths and principles " that might be supposed to militate against it.

So the other passage in Lev. xxv: 44–46, which has been supposed to refer to the enslavement of foreigners by the Jews—and which does so refer, if any passage in the Mosaic code does—is a *direct* and *positive* regulation, instituting, by express and direct enactment, for the Jews, and granting to them *the right to do forever* that which is therein spoken of and provided for. Do read this statute too, patient reader. " Both thy bondmen and thy bondmaids, which thou shalt have, shall be of the heathen that are round about you; of them shall ye buy bondmen and bondmaids. Moreover, of the children of the strangers that do sojourn among you, of them shall ye buy, and of their families that are with you, which they begat in your land; and they shall be your possession: And ye shall take them as an inheritance for your children after you, to inherit them for a possession; they shall be your bondmen forever." Nothing can be more direct and positive.

Nothing can be plainer than that what is here enacted was expressly made a *permanent law* of the Jewish economy. If the thing enacted was "*slavery*," then we have, in this passage, express and positive institution of slavery, as a permanent arrangement, by divine authority and with direct divine sanction, and so put forever beyond the reach of the effect of great abstract "truths and principles." There is not one characteristic of merely "restraining and regulating" legislation in this whole statute: but every mark of direct and positive enactment, expressly instituting and rendering permanent that which is enacted. If that thing is "*slavery*," then the Bible does institute, establish, and sanction slavery.

More than this, even. If this statute relates to slavery, it is both a constituting and *an anticipatory* law. It was a law in advance of the existence of that which is enacted by the law. For Moses expressly says, (Gen. xlvi: 27,) "All the souls of the house of Jacob which came into Egypt were three score and fifteen souls." Stephen, Acts vii: 14, describes these as "*kindred*." Surely, therefore, no one will pretend that there were *foreign slaves* in Jacob's household when he and his family went down into Egypt. So, after the Israelites were in Egypt, from Joseph to Moses, there is not the least shadow of evidence that they held foreign slaves, or any other slaves. Indeed, one great object of Divine Providence in permitting them to be "oppressed" in Egypt, was to teach them to abhor all oppression and all unrighteous bondage, and to "know the heart of the stranger." It is preposterous in the extreme, not to say shockingly blasphemous, to suppose that Moses led out of Egypt a great company of slave-holders, with a gang of slaves at their heels; and that while God poured out his terrible judgments upon the Egyptians for treating the Jews as slaves, he, at the same moment, protected the Jews in the perpetration of precisely the same crime! The Jews, then, came out of Egypt free from foreign slaves— free from slaves of all sorts—free from slavery. This law, therefore, in Leviticus, *did not* find any "slavery in existence established by law" to regulate. Hence, if it relates to slavery, it is both an originating, instituting enactment, and an enactment in anticipation. It positively establishes that which did not previously exist.

The assumption, therefore, that slavery is nowhere expressly instituted or approved in the Bible, is entirely incorrect, *provided this law in Leviticus relates to slavery*. But the argument under consideration takes it for granted that it does relate to slavery. If it does relate to slavery, then it expressly established it, and made it permanent, among the Jews forever.

If, on the other hand, this law does not relate to slavery, then all this talk about Moses's "regulating and restraining" slavery is irrelevant and idle. It was something else that he regulated, and not slavery: something that would bear to be established, approved, and made permanent by the positive legislation of the Almighty.

If this legislation relates to free, righteous servitude, as we think we have fully shown that it does, with all propriety it might be express, positive, and permanent.

But the theological teaching in this view of Bible treatment of chattel slavery is open to very serious objections. It admits that slavery is an evil, a moral wrong that ought not to exist, that ought to be repented of and abandoned, wherever it does exist. It also represents the Bible as holding a parley with it, avoiding much direct mention of it, and seeking, in an indirect way, its gradual abandonment. So far as all this applies to individual slaveholding, we regard it very bad theology indeed. We do not believe that the "wise and scriptural" way of breaking off any form of sin whatever, is by gentle degrees. We do not think that the sin of chattelizing human beings is such a privileged sort of iniquity, that the Bible is content to have people "roll it as a sweet morsel under the tongue" very leisurely awhile, as if to dissolve it away very gently and gradually. We do not judge that it is either the doctrine or the policy of the Bible that people should taper off any kind of sin by convenient degrees. We seem to hear it thundering its mighty maledictions of death and damnation across the pathway of every poor sinner, warning him to take

24

another step in the transgressor's path at his peril, and we can not think that it only asks of the wretch who robs his fellows of his Adamic and God-given manhood, and degrades him to a mere piece of property, to repent very "gradually," and to stop his high-handed and heaven-daring wickedness little by little, spinning out the final issue into some indefinite period of future time. This looks to us like a gross slander upon God's Bible and its theological teaching.

In our view, the Bible does meet and grapple directly with chattel slavery, classing it, with terrible brevity and significance, among capital crimes.

With similar directness, all oppression of common, or unchattelized servants, is everywhere met, denounced, and forbidden, in the strongest language. Throughout both Testaments, all trespass upon manhood rights, whether in the shape of slavery or any thing else, is met face to face, with the sternest maledictions. Not a particle of this sort of iniquity is "regulated," but the whole of it is denounced and forbidden. It is simply flat untruth to assert that the Bible treats it in a very "gentle," "bland," and indirect manner.

Take a single example of Bible dealing with oppression, which is the Bible word for all trespass upon personal and inalienable rights. "The people of the land have used oppression, and exercised robbery, and have vexed the poor and needy. Yea, they have oppressed the stranger wrongfully. Therefore, have I poured out mine indignation upon them; I have consumed them with the fire of my wrath."— Ezek. xxii: 29. How *plain* and *direct* the charge here! If the wickedness complained of here had reached the horrid depth of slaveholding outright, how strong and faithful the description! There is no circumlocution, no softening of terms, no dodging lest somebody's negro-hating "prejudices" should be disturbed. The charge is direct, positive, strong, and emphatic. And then how terrible the threatening that follows! "I have CONSUMED them with the *fire of my wrath!*" FIRE OF GOD'S WRATH! CONSUMED with that fearful fire! And shall we be told, in the very same breath, that the Bible way of treating this same iniquity is very "gentle," and "kind," and "bland," and indirect, as if, like many, too many modern teachers, it feared to disturb the "existing prejudices" or feelings of some perpetrator of this abominable crime?

There never was a more miserable and shallow delusion than this: that the Bible treats slaveholding oppression, or any other form of oppression, very tenderly. Why, it is enough to make one's blood run chill to read the denunciations of the Bible on this subject. They pervade the whole Bible.

Slavery, as a system, is not denounced; for that would mean nothing: but all trespass upon personal and manhood rights, whether in the shape of slaveholding, or any thing else, is everywhere forbidden and denounced, but never *regulated*. The Bible does not regulate iniquity, but forbids it. It denounces eternal death upon it. It demands immediate repentance. Our God is a direct, terrible, and "swift witness" against all sin, and especially "against those that oppress the hireling in his wages, the widow and the fatherless, and that turn aside the stranger from his right."

THE END.